Hispanic Theatre in the United States

Edited by
Nicolás Kanellos

Arte Público Press
Houston
1984

Hispanic Theatre in the United States is made possible through a grant from the National Endowment for the Humanities.

Arte Público Press
Revista Chicano-Riqueña
University of Houston
Houston, Texas 77004

Printed in the United States of America

Acknowledgements

We would like to express our appreciation to the following libraries and special collections that have rescued Hispanic materials and made them accessible to us for the exhibit, "Two Centuries of Hispanic Theatre in the United States," and this book:

Bancroft Collection, University of California-Berkeley
Benson Latin American Collection, University of Texas at Austin
Billy Rose Theatre Collection, New York Public Library, Lincoln Center
Chicano Studies Library, University of California-Los Angeles
Chicano Studies Library, University of California-Berkeley
Houston Metropolitan Archives, Houston Public Library
Mexican American Studies Project, Benson Latin American Library, University of Texas at Austin
San Antonio Conservation Society
Southwest Museum, Los Angeles
Special Collections, Library, University of Miami
Tampa Public Library
University of Southern Florida Library

The following individuals and organizations provided materials, support, and expertise:

Rosita Avella (University of Miami Library), Leonardo García Astol, Susie Mijares Astol, Belia Areu Camargo, Carmen Cubas, Lupita Fernández, Galindo Real Estate (San Antonio), Francisco García, Cindy Garza, Soledad Godínez, Arturo Gómez, Jorge Huerta, José G. González, René and María Gonzales (Spanish Little Theatre, Tampa), William Lansford, Librería Española (San Antonio), Raúl A. López, Lydia Mendoza, Mexican American Studies, University of Texas (San Antonio), Narciso Peña, Tony Pizzo, Elsa Ortiz Robles (Robles Communications, New York), F. Arturo Rosales, Rafael Trujillo Herrera, and Tomás Ybarra-Frausto.

Very special thanks to Francisco Blasco, coordinator and curator of the national touring exhibit of "Two Centuries of Hispanic Theatre in the United States," sponsored by the National Endowment for the Humanities and the University of Houston.

Contents

Illustrated promptbook used by the Hernández-Villalongín company in the Southwest, late nineteenth and early twentieth centuries. (Benson Library, University of Texas)

Nicolás Kanellos
University of Houston

An Overview of Hispanic Theatre in the United States

The history of Hispanic theatre north of the Rio Grande begins with the improvised dramas of the colonizers in Juan de Oñate's expedition to New Mexico in 1598. The colonizers, as well as the missionaries that followed in subsequent expeditions, planted the roots of both secular and religious folk drama that are still bearing fruit today in the form of the shepherds plays or *pastorelas* which are performed during the Christmas season.

The origins of the professional stage in the Southeast, however, go back to the early nineteenth century when troupes of Mexican and Spanish performers began touring the port cities of California and northern Mexico. By mid-century, such companies as Gerardo López del Castillo's Compañía Española traveled a firmly established circuit along the Pacific Coast by steamship from Mazatlán up to San Diego, Los Angeles and San Francisco, from Baja California across the Gulf of Baja and inland by stage coach to northern towns in Mexico and up to Tucson.[1]

The 1840s and 1850s witnessed the construction of many theatre houses in Los Angeles and San Francisco, as well as the use of inns and private homes for Spanish-language theatrical performances by subscription. Many of these establishments, like the theatre built in 1848 as an addition to the house of Antonio F. Coronel, future mayor of Los Angeles, housed both Spanish- and English-language companies.[2]

By the time the first Anglo-American theatres and the first minstrels began settling in, the Hispanic stage had already set down deep roots and was serving as entertainment and high culture for Spanish and non-Spanish speakers. Also, such venerable cultural institutions as the opera in San Francisco can trace their lineage back to Hispanic origins. According to McGroarty, "The first grand opera in the State of Califor-

7

nia was in 1847 when the Alvarez Opera Company came from Lima, Peru, on a lumber vessel, lured to the camp of San Francisco by the magnificent subscription of $10,000."[3]

During the 1860s, López del Castillo's company became a resident theatre in San Francisco, where it not only presented melodramas by Spanish, Mexican and Cuban authors, but it also served as a focus and catalyst for Mexican community affairs. López del Castillo and his company served to reenforce the language and culture of Mexicans and other Hispanics in San Francisco in the face of increasing pressure from Anglo-American immigration. López del Castillo also served as president of the Junta Patriótica Mexicana de San Francisco and placed his company at the service of the community, with benefit performances even to raise funds for Juarez' liberation forces and the widowed and orphaned of the Franco-Mexican War.[4] The social and political involvement of López del Castillo's company exemplifies the relationship of the Hispanic stage to the community throughout its history in the United States.

By the 1890s, the Hispanic stage was developing in other areas of the United States, areas which were soon becoming a basis for a theatrical circuit. Laredo—San Antonio—El Paso in Texas became the heart of an itinerary for troupes coming up from interior Mexico to tour along the border. With the Mexican Revolution and the massive exodus of all social segments that it produced, the major cities in the Southwest and Midwest became Mexican population centers that demanded entertainments comparable to those previously offered in Mexico City and Guadalajara. The theatres also reinforced the Spanish language and Hispanic customs and values in an alien surrounding. By the 1920s, all major and smaller cities in the Southwest supported theatre houses and became part of a circuit traveled by train and auto from Texas to California.

The 1890s also saw the enthusiastic creation of a Hispanic theatre in Tampa by the Spanish and Cuban owners of cigar factories who had relocated from Cuba because of the turmoil of the Cuban War of Independence, to circumvent U.S. import taxes and to get closer to their markets on the United States mainland. Within a period of fifteen years, the tobacco entrepeneurs built more than five grandiose, fully-equipped theatres in their mutualist halls in order to entertain all segments of Tampa-Ybor City society with performances by professional touring companies from Spain and Cuba. Many of these made their way northward on an itinerary that began in Key West, Florida, and terminated in New York.

While New York, since the 1820s, served as a publications center for Hispanic literature and theatre, the professional Spanish-language stage did not really get under way until the second decade of the

El Centro Español theatre in Ybor City, constructed in 1892.

Interior, El Centro Español theatre.

twentieth century. The Midwest also began to develop a stage, for the most part semi-professional and amateur, in the 1920s, but also housed the professional companies on tour from the East to the Southwest.

The true flourishing of Spanish-language theatre occurs in the 1920s,[5] with Los Angeles and San Antonio supporting more than twenty houses that were showing everything from melodrama and *zarzuela* to vaudeville, and with tent theatres traveling to smaller towns and cities throughout the five southwestern states. In Los Angeles there appeared more than thirty playwrights, some of whom were successful in basing their plays on Hispanic life in the United States, particularly the Mexican background of California and the epic of the immigration produced by the Mexican Revolution. The vaudevillians and the playwrights who wrote satirical *revistas* (short one-act burlesques with music and comedy) reconsidered over and over again life in the urban communities of the United States, two languages and two cultures in conflict, and a newly emerging Mexican-American identity. Theatrical professionals from throughout the Hispanic world were drawn to Los Angeles, the center of the motion picture industry for the United States and Latin America. The pool of talent drawn for the movies enriched live theatre immeasurably. In fact, Hispanic impresarios and directors from throughout the United States and northern Mexico would come to Los Angeles to recruit talent for new touring companies.

In the 1920s, New York and Tampa also experienced a flourishing that linked their theatre houses to those of Madrid and Havana, with

This full house attests to the popularity of theatrical entertainment in the Puerto Rican community in the '40s.

Spanish melodrama and Spanish *zarzuela* taking the lead in popularity, only to accede to working-class demands for Cuban *teatro bufo* by the close of the decade. The Cuban's burlesques revolved around set characters like *el negrito* in black face, *la mulata* and *el gallego* (Galician) and incorporated the increasingly popular Afro-Cuban music and dance.

For the most part, the Midwest did not develop its own resident professional companies and Spanish-language theatre houses, but it did have extensive amateur activity and it did support professional companies touring from the East and Southwest. Various amateur companies, however, were created and directed by professionals from the Mexico City stage. In Indiana Harbor/East Chicago, Indiana, the Cuadro Dramático del Círculo de Obreros Católicos San José was such a company. Under the directorship of J. Jesús Cabrera, and as a wholesome fundraising and cultural activity associated with Our Lady of Guadalupe Church, the Círculo de Obreros Católicos and mutual aid societies, the Cuadro Dramático was truly remarkable in its high level of professionalism and popularity, often producing the same plays running concurrently on stages in Mexico City.

The Great Depression devastated Hispanic theatre in the Southwest and Midwest, as the communities were depopulated through forced and voluntary repatriation to Mexico. Hollywood moguls quickly bought out many of the theatres housing Hispanic productions and converted them for talking motion pictures. The theatrical artists from the Southwest who wanted to practice their profession had three options:

The Tampa Federal Theatre Project with Director Manuel Aparicio at center.

Tampa Federal Theatre rehearsal of *El Hijo Pródigo* at the Centro Asturiano.

(1) return to Mexico and eke out a living there; (2) stay on in the Southwest and place their art at the service of the church and community charities, but give up hopes of making a living from the stage; (3) or move to New York where the growing influx of Puerto Ricans during the Depression and war years gave them a second life on the stage, principally as vaudevillians. A few other artists were able to land jobs in Spanish-language radio and the small tent theatres that toured the border.

One of the Southwestern stars who achieved great popularity on the New York stage and, thereafter, in Cuba and Puerto Rico, was the great comedienne Beatriz "La Chata" Noloesca. There she shared the stage with Cuban, Puerto Rican, Argentine and other Hispanic performers at such houses as the Teatro Hispano and El Teatro Puerto Rico well into the 1950s. The Teatro Hispano maintained its box office sales and outlasted the Depression by appealing especially to working-class audiences. It supported and housed community affairs, fund-raisers, turkey-raffles and talent contests.

The only Hispanic company to be supported by the WPA's Federal Theatre Project during the Depression was the Tampa company. Under the direction of Manuel Aparicio, also of the New York stage, the company performed some of the stock *zarzuelas* and melodramas from the Hispanic repertoire, as well as works translated to Spanish and prescribed by the Federal Theatre. The "Cuban Company," as it was known in the WPA, also opened Sinclair Lewis' *It Can Happen Here* at the same time that Federal Theatre companies around the country did.

The postwar period in the Southwest has seen the gradual restoration of the amateur, semiprofessional and professional stages in the Hispanic communities of the Southwest. From the 1950s on, repertory theatres have appeared throughout the Southwest and Midwest to produce Latin American, Spanish and American plays in Spanish translation.

But the most remarkable story of the stage in the Southwest is that of the spontaneous appearance in 1965 of a labor theatre in the agricultural fields, under the directorships of Luis Valdez, and its creation of a full-blown theatrical movement that conquered the hearts and minds of artists and activists throughout the country. Under the leadership of Valdez' El Teatro Campesino, for more than a decade Chicano theatres dramatized the political and cultural concerns of their communities while criss-crossing the states on tour. The movement, largely student- and worker-based, eventually led to professionalization, Hollywood and Broadway productions and the creation of the discipline of Chicano theatre at universities.

With greater professionalization and the transition of Chicano theatre people into mainstream entertainment and the universities, and with the abatement of the civil rights movement, the grass-roots theatre movement has subsided. Today there are more repertory theatre companies performing conventional Latin American plays than there are Chicano theatre groups. Many of these repertories are increasingly supported by funds from public arts agencies, the latter rarely having supported the more politicized Chicano theatres. Among the most important achievements have been the creation of Carmen Zapata's Bilingual Theatre Foundation as a showcase of Hispanic talent for Hollywood, the expansion of El Teatro Campesino into the motion picture business and the survival of El Teatro de la Esperanza as a national touring company.

In 1983, Tampa celebrated the twenty-fifth anniversary of the Spanish Repertory Theatre, the inheritor of the illustrious theatrical tradition which began almost a century ago. To date, the theatre continues to produce *zarzuela*, Cuban *zarzuela*, dramas from the Hispanic world, and Broadway musicals, like *Fiddler on the Roof*, in translation. Farther South, in Miami, the last two decades have seen the development of another Hispanic theatre center, concommitant with the growth of Miami's Cuban population. To date, a theatre expressly reflecting Cuban-American life in Miami and Tampa has not appeared. But the production of Spanish and Latin American works, as well as those of the Cuban exile theatre, have been accomplished with great artistry and professionalism.

Today New York offers the largest number and the broadest range of Hispanic theatre companies. It lays claim to one national touring company, El Teatro Repertorio Español; a major theatre in the Broadway

New York's Teatro 4.

An outdoor performance of *El pagador de promesas* in 1974 by the Puerto Rican Traveling Theatre.

district, Miriam Colón's Puerto Rican Traveling Theatre; a number of very stable off-Broadway houses like INTAR; and even an improvisational collective in the tradition of Chicano theatre and Latin American popular theatre, Teatro 4. Noteworthy too is the development of a group of Nuyorican playwrights, Puerto Rican writers who reflect the New York reality in predominantly English-language scripts. Chief among these is Miguel Piñero, winner of the Obie and New York Drama Critics Circle Award for his play, *Short Eyes*. Another prize winner—who joins Piñero in seeing his prize-winning play made into a feature film—is Iván Acosta, author of *El Super*, a bittersweet comedy of Cuban immigration to New York. Both the Puerto Rican and the Cuban American theatres seem to have healthy beginnings in New York and augur major contributions to the American stage.

[1] See my article, "El teatro profesional hispánico: Orígenes en el Suroeste, *La Palabra*" 2/1 (1980), 16-24.

[2] See my article, "Nineteenth-Century Origins of the Hispanic Theatre in the Southwest," *Crítica*, 1/1 (1984).

[3] John Steven McGroarty, *Los Angeles From the Mountains to the Sea* (Chicago and New York: the American Historical Society, 1921), Vol. 1, p. 378.

[5] See my article, "The Flourishing of Hispanic Theatre in the Southwest," *Latin American Theatre Review* 16/1 (Fall, 1983), 29-40.

Circo Escalante Hnos.

COMPAÑIA DE BAILE Y VARIEDADES

Carpas Situadas en el extremo oeste de la calle Congress

Hoy- Martes 29 de Marzo-Hoy

Regia Funcion de Gracia --- Notable Acontecimiento

LO MEJOR DE LO MEJOR

Funcion de Beneficio

Predomina la Nobleza, Predomina el Humanitarismo

¡Ojo!   ¡Ojo!   ¡Ojo!

AL PUBLICO

Habiendo ocurrido el comité "Grijalva" el que encargado está para colectar fondos de la hospitalaria colonia mexicana, con objeto de llevar hasta el fin la defensa judicial de un hermano de raza, ha ocurrido, repito, a la compañía Escalante Hnos., solicitando encarecidamente, de dicha empresa, una función de gracia, función de beneficio, para fortalecer más los fondos destinados a tan noble y humanitaria acción, los hermanos Escalante, sin poner objeción alguna, gustosos y satisfechos de tan digno proceder, han accedido orgullosos de poder contribuir con su pequeño grano de arena y al mismo tiempo cumplir con un deber sagrado.

ALFREDO GRIJALVA

Esperamos del amable y benévolo público que nos favorece, ocurran a esta simpática velada que tiene por objeto tan noble y magnánimo principio; no dudamos que el público tucsonense siempre se ha distinguido por su caritativo proceder, y por lo mismo, recordamos no olvidar que tan enorme pena puede acabar la vida de una amable esposa y amabilísimos hijos que deja tras sí a sufrir inexplicables peripecias. Anticipamos las más debidas gracias a todo aquel que pudiera prestar una mano ayudadora a quien tanto lo necesita.

ESCALANTE HNOS.   COMITE "GRIJALVA."

Trapecios -- Barras -- Alambristas -- Bailes -- Cantos
Couplet, Zarzuela, Recitaciones, Excentricos y Pantomimas esta Noche.
No Faltando los Siempre Graciosos y Ocurrentes "Cara Sucia," "Tony" y "Chamaco."
Al Circo esta Noche a Contribuir con tan Noble Cometido

PRECIOS DE ENTRADA

Entrada General	50c
Niños	25c
Asientos Reservados -- Ex.	25c

Poster, Circo Escalante.

F. Arturo Rosales
Arizona State University

Spanish-Language Theatre and Early Mexican Immigration

One of the best kept secrets in American cultural history is that theatre and other forms of live entertainment have had a long and vibrant tradition in the Hispanic community of the United States. In recent years, however, the historical phenomenon of Spanish-language theatre has been rescued from obscurity by a diverse group of researchers. Using traditional historical research techniques, Tomás Ybarra-Frausto, Nicolás Kanellos, Armando Miguélez and Jorge Huerta, among others, scoured archives, old newspapers and other sources in Mexico and the United States to piece together a remarkably detailed chronicle of live Spanish-language theatre and the people associated with it.[1] Mexican-style vaudeville, classical drama, circuses and musical revues were an integral feature of Hispanic communities in the nineteenth-century Southwest and mushrooming immigrant barrios of the twentieth century. In fact, such activity was supported by the Hispanic public long after mass media curtailed the phenomenon in mainstream society.

The work of these scholars, although still in its seminal stages, has yielded a rich texture which should be further woven into the general historical experience of Hispanics in the United States before we can have a complete understanding of how the medium functioned in the community. The purpose of this essay is to provide a theoretical framework from which Spanish-language theatre can be analyzed vis-a-vis its value within the total Mexican community in the United States.

Oscar Handlin, a pioneer historian of immigration and ethnicity in the United States, provided essential theoretical constructs regarding the process of adaptation for ethnic groups. He concluded that immigrant culture and other ethnic institutions retarded entry into America's mainstream. He felt that the immigrant's background was not adequate to demands made of them in the new industrial environment of the

United States and that the psychological security found in an ethnic enclave was not worth the price paid in retarded Americanization, preventing full participation in the opportunity structure of the United States.[2]

Handlin's work has served a whole generation of scholars and while much of his positing has intrinsic value, social historians have taken issue with the notion that ethnic institutions are necessarily an obstacle to successful adaptation and economic or social mobility. Ethnic community, in fact, has provided some of the main avenues of success for its members.[3] Political patronage, small businesses and even professional success were dependent on ethnic identity. An Italian lawyer or doctor, for example, found his old neighborhood the most propitious place for his practice. Moreover, his very education might have been financed by a society of Italian American workers banding together initially for their own mutual aid, eventually transcending initial objectives by helping some of their children achieve higher educational status.

Perhaps the most important and positive feature in the formation of the ethnic community, however, is the manner in which social networking allowed the regular members to interact within the larger society. This is why scholars of immigration have found the study of interlocking institutions so crucial to understanding how immigrant societies function. Social scientists have analyzed the various components of ethnic communities, such as language, mutual aid/recreation societies, family, religion, newspapers, entrepreneurship, and the work place to assess whether immigrant institutions have been functional or dysfunctional in helping newcomers adapt to their new environment. Theater and live entertainment, focused in the immigrant communities themselves, obviously played an important role within this social networking. Interlaced within the immigrant church, various ethnic organizations, the business community and class structure, theatrical performances served as a cohesive force.[4]

These generalizations, concerning not just theatre, but also the functions and networking process of immigrant institutions, apply to the Mexican immigrant community as well. However, there are some significant differences between the general immigrant experience in the United States and that of Mexicans. When massive immigration to the Southwest in response to industrial development began in the latter part of the nineteenth century, the area already contained a vibrant Hispanic culture. Mexican cultural institutions, left over from the time the Southwest belonged to Mexico, were maintained and reinforced because of continuing ties with that country. Such aspects of Spanish-language theatre as *pastorelas,* which dated to the colonial period, and modern theatre, were already integrated into this southwestern milieu when massive immigration expanded the scope of Hispanic society.[5]

Approximately one hundred thousand Mexicans lived in the territories, that as a result of the Texas Rebellion (1836), the Mexican-American War (1846), and the Gadsden Purchase (1853) became part of the United States. The Southwest remained pastoral and basically pre-industrial until a railroad network connecting this isolated region with the more developed parts of the United States dramatically altered the economy of the area. The same impetus which forged the network in the Southwest also extended into Mexico. By the 1890s, countless trains laden with iron ore, copper, coal and commercial agricultural products steamed into industrial centers in midwestern and northeastern America from northern Mexico and the Southwest, fueling the industrial expansion of these areas. From Mexico, these very same trains also brought, between 1880 and 1930, hundreds of thousands of Mexican workers and their families whose labor was essential to the new economy.

Following the network of economic development, the majority of the immigrants initially went to Texas where they swelled already existent communities of native Southwest Mexicans. In cities like El Paso and San Antonio, and in countless Rio Grande Valley communities, they labored in agriculture, textile plants and smelters. Similarly Arizona, California and southern New Mexico quickly acquired immigrant barrios as Mexican workers responded to recruitment efforts by agriculture, mining and railroad interests. Numerous new towns sprang up in Arizona and southern California as reclamation projects transformed dry desert regions into fertile gardens. As early as 1930, Los Angeles had become the largest Mexican community outside of Mexico City and every major city in the Southwest had large teeming *colonias*. By 1930 the tide of Mexican immigration had also surged to the United States North and had even penetrated Canada and Alaska. Chicago and Detroit, however, were the main recipients of this influx outside of the Southwest and Chicago, in fact, acquired one of the largest urban concentrations in the country.[6]

Development of ethnic culture in the *colonias* reflected the exigencies and environs of the host communities. *Barrios* were shaped by such variants as physical configurations of neighborhoods, the kind of work performed by the immigrants, and nuances like the ratio of men to women. Obviously Chicago *barrios* would take on distinctions not found in agricultural communities in South Texas. Still all Mexican *colonias* had more in common with each other than differences, and one institution that ran through all the immigrant barrios, ranking up front with the Church and ethnic organizations was theatre. This activity existed everywhere, essentially because troupes were mobile, able to take this medium into the most remote corners where Mexicans lived and worked. Caliber, size and genre of the medium determined where these traveling groups would go. Los Angeles, San Antonio and other large cities were preferable to the more professional groups such as La Compañía de Virginia Fábregas, directed by one of Latin America's most renowned actresses, Virginia Fábregas, because of their large population and palatial theatrical houses. Dusty agricultural communities and mining towns were catered to by smaller tent-show ensembles, which were called "Carpas," usually consisting of a nuclear family of versatile performers, who put on humorous skits supplemented by tight-wire walking and other circus-like acts.[7]

These distinctions can be carried too far because many high quality acts reached remote regions and the "Carpa" performers would sign up as an individual vaudeville act with impresarios in large cities. The net impact was the same regardless of where the Mexican *colonias* were located. In addition to actors, many traveling troupes included musicians and folkloric dancers. All of these live performances, regardless of their nature, inspired local imitations and, as they traveled across Hispanic United States, they left a residue of amateur *cuadros dramáticos*, *orquestas típicas* and folkloric dance groups.

Theatre required not only physical space, which in most communities served as a focus of community similar to church buildings, pool halls and merchant shops, but it also created a psychological dependency as mass media does today. There is a major qualitative difference, however, between theatre activity as it affected Hispanics during the initial formation of the *colonias* and films, television, records and radio today. Theatrical performances assisted in local networking, interacting and intertwining with the other barrio institutions to provide cohesion and stability in a way that contemporary mass media, even that which is geared to the Hispanic public, cannot do.[8]

Church plays, for example, had didactic goals. The anniversary of the appearance of Our Virgin of Guadalupe to Juan Diego was marked annually on December 12 by plays depicting the event. Similarly, other religious holidays were celebrated with dramatic presentations such as observations of Holy Week in which *matachines* (religious dancers) acted out imaginary battles between the Christians and Moors. At a time before the gadgetry and sophisticated techniques of modern electronic media dulled the ability of live entertainment to enthrall and captivate audiences, dramatic religious events left lasting impressions among churchgoers, reinforcing loyalty and faith to religious teachings.[9]

Furthermore, theatrical activity integrated Mexican investors into community activity. Arranging vaudeville, circus and popular theatre was a supreme entrepreneurial opportunity for Mexican immigrant merchants. In essence, ethnic businessmen were more successful when they marketed goods and services that non-Mexican merchants could not provide or were not interested in providing. This left for the Mexican immigrant entrepreneur a market vacuum in such areas as processing ethnic food, importing commodities from Mexico, restauranting, tailoring clothing to specific ethnic tastes, Spanish-language printing and publishing, and of course, providing recreation and entertainment. Sometimes for no other reason than a profit motive, Mexican immigrant businessmen expanded their interests into the entertainment area. The Sarabia family in Houston, for example, whose initial capital came from contracting immigrant laborers to the Southern Pacific Railroad during the 1920s, ventured into retailing groceries, curios, records and sheet music, and eventually they opened up the Azteca Theater in 1928, which featured theatrical performances, vaudeville, and silent films.[10]

In Tucson *El Teatro Carmen* was established in 1915 by Carmen Soto de Vásquez, the wife of a local merchant. The theatre was a financial success, but it is clear Señora Soto de Vásquez in her efforts was impelled to patronize the arts by motives other than profit. As Armando Miguélez has indicated in his study of theatre in Tucson, "Carmen Soto de Vásquez was conscious of her role as a culture promoter who put the theatre at the disposal of the public so they would have the opportunity to enjoy art characteristic of their culture and so that by supporting . . . these events, culture [Mexican], would be retained in the city."[11]

Drama, especially of the high art variety, resulted in catharsis for the amateur actors and promoters of this form, most of whom came from the middle class of the immigrant community. During the Mexican Revolution, thousands of middle and upper class refugees, forced to flee Mexico, were consequently torn from a social milieu which afforded prestige and reinforced their image as "gente decente." As refugees in the United States they lost little time in recreating class distinctions. Some refugees were able to bring capital, others skills and, for those whose fortunes were lost, gracious speech and manners set them off from their more working-class compatriots in the barrios. Within this framework, participation in artistic activity became an important vehicle for reasserting identity and image projection. Legitimate theatre provided an opportunity for amateurs to mix with professionals and for some, the events presented an opportunity for social mobility. In the unstable class structure of the barrios, young Mexicans from the "gente humilde" could rub shoulders with people who in Mexico would have been out of their social strata.[12]

Perhaps one of the most interesting functions of live entertainment was the manner in which it was weaved into the political life of the community. The first political issues of Mexicans in the United States concerned the subordination of native Mexicans who were left in the United States after partition of the Southwest from Mexico. Then as immigration increased, adjustment to a new environment and all of the attendant problems involved in this process—alienation, rejection by the host community, and abuse in the workplace—became paramount.

19

As *colonias* matured and as the immigrants and their offspring acquired more experience, they tackled these problems as all other immigrant groups have: by organizing labor unions, civil rights groups and by insisting they be accommodated into the host society.[13]

Initially, however, political action in the immigrant community consisted of creating techniques to survive in an alien and indifferent environment rooted in *laissez-faire* principles. Thus benevolent societies were organized to provide mutual security to individuals during hard times. These same organizations sometimes also provided relief from cultural alienation, a problem so severe that if ignored resulted in anomic behavior. Since Anglo institutions were not relevant to the experience of the immigrants and more often Mexicans were not allowed to participate in mainstream cultural activity, identity and positive self-image had to be generated in the barrios. Mutual aid societies often doubled as recreation clubs using Mexican cultural activity, usually live theatrical entertainment, as the main source of inspiration. Seen in this context theatre was political in nature.

Very early in the experience of both native Mexicans and immigrants, theatre and live performances were used for more direct political impact. During the 1860s, for example, Gerardo López del Castillo staged plays in San Francisco, California, to raise funds for the Republican cause in Mexico during the French Intervention. More often, theatre served to raise funds for persons who were, from the perspective of the community, wrongly accused of crimes and at the same time plays written especially for these events dramatized the victim's dilemma. The film, *The Ballad of Gregorio Cortez*, which concerns the most famous case of this kind, has a scene depicting a fundraiser in which actors on stage motivate the crowd to donate money by recreating the ordeal of Cortez who led Sheriff's posses and Texas Rangers on an eight-day chase through South Texas after Cortez.

Just as dramatic was the case of Aurelio Pompa, a Mexican immigrant from Sonora who shot and killed his foreman at a Los Angeles work site in 1921 in an incident which the Mexican community considered self-defense. Theatre played a more prominent role in this event. As in the Cortez episode, a *corrido* was composed about the ordeal, but in addition a structured play depicting the event was also written and performed to raise money for his defense and it was still playing after Pompa was executed.[14]

Theatrics and live entertainment were used in numerous other cases to raise funds for issues similar to the Cortez and Pompa incidents. In 1921, for instance, two Mexicans, on death row at New York's Sing Sing prison captured the attention of Mexican communities throughout the United States, and in San Antonio the *Brigada Cruz Azul*, a young ladies organization, raised funds for their defense by staging a play. In

Gerardo López del Castillo.

Tucson, in 1927, the *Circo Escalante*, one of the most well know circuses in the United States, was brought into town to help offset the legal fees of Alfredo Grijalva, an immigrant convicted of killing a border patrol agent in a case that was so full of legal errors that the judge even admitted that Grijalva should not have gone to jail. [15]

In sum, theatre in general served to reinforce ritual observations of holidays, weekends and reinforced cultural values, providing demonstrations of correct or incorrect behavior. For a public hungry to see itself reflected on stage, the influence of drama in shaping values, attitudes and more general outlook on life can not be overestimated. However, not all theatrical performances were relevent to the every day life of the immigrant community. Nicolás Kanellos relates how during the 1920s, cost-conscious impresarios in Los Angeles preferred classical Spanish plays over recently written works about the immigrant experience because classical pieces could be obtained from well-worn books and using them did not require royalties. Increasingly, however, plays and vaudeville comedy routines and songs contained material about immigrant life. One motiff, as has already been indicated, was related to inequities in the justice system, but other styles concerned Mexicans who put on airs, became Anglicized, who suffered indignities at the hands of Anglos or who lapsed into moral turpitude.[16]

Spanish-language live entertainment in the United States, as it is in all industrialized and urbanized nations, has declined as a commercial venture. Some exceptions, such as the phenomenal success of "Zoot Suit" in Los Angeles, demonstrates that there is an interest if the drama has the high appeal of that work. After the 1920s, the advent of films, especially the Mexican film, came to overshadow live entertainment, even though theatres, as late as the 1950s, screened films alongside live performers. Television, of course, has removed even further, the mainstream population from live entertainment. Although it is not understood whether Spanish-language electronic media can have functions similar to its predecessors among the large population of recent immigrants from Mexico and other parts of Latin America, it is clear that the direct physical contact of earlier entertainment is not there.[17]

The absence of direct participation of immigrants and their institutions in their entertainment has important ramifications in the present day. What is most obvious is that they cannot deal with issues and problems which at one time were addressed through this medium. This of course is a tentative assessment. Since the function of live performances were never politically radical, and deeply rooted in traditional values, one can envision that the more far-reaching effects of Spanish-language electronic media can create advertising opportunities for larger ethnic enterprises and serve to create mild nationalistic awareness serving Hispanic politicians. Ultimately the media can help Hispanics acquire a power base within the status quo political and economic structure of the United States. This would be a continuation of the more localized but similar function of earlier entertainment.

[1] See Nicolás Kanellos, ed., *Mexican American Theatre: Then and Now* (Houston: Arte Publico Press, 1983), for a collection of this scholars' writings.

[2] Most of Handlin's ideas on immigration and ethnicity are contained in his classic work, *The Uprooted: The Epic Story of the Great Migrations That Made the American People* (Boston: Little, Brown and Company, 1973).

[3] See Rudolph Vecoli, "Contadini In Chicago: A Critique of *The Uprooted*," *Journal of American History*, 5 (Summer, 1964), 405-417, for the first major revision to Handlin's work. Since then, most social historians have followed Vecoli's lead regarding immigrant communities.

[4] See Timothy L. King, "Religion and Ethnicity in America," *The American Historical Review* 83 (December, 1978), 1115-1185, for a comprehensive view of religion as an instrument in social networking. What is ultimately important in this work is the review of the historical literature that treats networking in more general terms.

[5] Kanellos, "Two Centuries of Hispanic Theater in the Southwest," in *Mexican American Theatre*, 17-40.

[6] Numerous monographs and articles depicting the formation of Mexican immigrant communities have been produced in recent years. The best synthesis of these works is Rudolfo Acuña, *Occupied America: A History of Chicanos* (New York: Harper and Row, 1982).

[7] The essay collection in Kanellos, ed., *Mexican American Theatre*, provides a good discussion of all these features of Spanish-language theater in the United States.

[8] Despite the extensive historical literature produced on Mexican immigration in recent years, few works have adequately addressed the role of culture as a tangible cohesive force. Mario T. García, *Desert Immigrants: The Mexicans of El Paso, 1880-1920* (New Haven: Yale University Press, 1982), pp. 197-282, provides the most comprehensive view of the role of culture in one community. Rosales and Simon, "The Mexican Immigrant Experience in the Urban Midwest: East Chicago, Indiana, 1919-1945," *Indiana Magazine of History*, 37 (December, 1981), 333-357, and Rosales, "Mexicans in Houston: The Struggle to Survive, 1908-1975," *Houston Review*, 3 (Summer, 1981), 224-248, also provide similar insights into this phenomenon.

[9] See Kanellos, "Two Centuries of Hispanic Theatre In the Southwest," 17-40, and Tomás Ybarra-Frausto, "La Chata Noloesca: Figura del Donaire," 41-51, in Kanellos, ed., *Mexican American Theatre*, for a development of theater genres.

[10] Rosales, "Mexicans in Houston," 230.

[11] Armando Miguélez, "El Teatro Carmen (1915-1923): Centro del Arte Escénico Hispano en Tucson," in Kanellos, ed., *Mexican American Theatre*, 52-57.

[12] *Ibid.*, Ybarra-Frausto, "La Chata Noloesca," 41; Rosales and Simon, "The Mexican Immigrant Experience In the Urban Midwest," 339-340; García, *Desert Immigrants*, 207-208.

[13] For a political history of Chicanos, see José A. Hernández, *Mutual Aid For Survival: The Case of the Mexican American* (Malibar, Florida: Krieger Publishing Company, 1983).

[14] See Américo Paredes, *"With a Pistol in His Hand:" A Border Ballad and Its Hero* (Austin: University of Texas Press, 1958) for a detailed account of the Cortez incident; Ricardo Romo, *East Los Angeles: A History of a Barrio* (Austin: University of Texas, 1983), pp. 158-159.

[15] I am presently preparing a book-length manuscript on the history of criminal justice and Mexican immigrants during 1900-1980. The evidence of using theatre for these purposes is overwhelming; see Kanellos, "The Flourishing of Hispanic Theatre in the Southwest," *Latin American Theatre Review* 16/1 (Fall, 1983), 29-40.

[16] *Ibid.*

[17] *Ibid.*; Roberta Orona-Cordova "Zoot Suit and the Pachuco Phenomenon: An Interview with Luis Valdez," *Mexican American Theater*, 95-111; Alex M. Saragoza, "Mexican Cinema In the United States, 1940-1952," in Mario García, *et. al.*, *History, Culture and Society: Chicano Culture in the 1980s* (Ypsilanti, Michigan: Bilingual Press, 1983), 107-124.

John C. Miller
New York University

Contemporary Hispanic Theatre in New York

In order to approach the contemporary circumstances or new trends of Hispanic theatre in New York, it seems necessary to outline its earlier history and fate. For those purposes, I am sketching the development of three periods of Hispanic theatre in New York which are delineated: Youth, 1917-1965; Adolescence, 1965-1977; Maturity, 1977 to the present.[1]

Hispanic theatre in New York had its beginning in the 1910s, principally through musical variety shows presented by touring Spanish, Cuban and European groups. The first New York-based professional Hispanic theatrical troupe, *La Compañía del teatro español,* produced eight plays (Alvarez Quintero, Benavente, Dicenta, Martínez Sierra and Muñoz Seca) during the 1921-22 theatrical season. As the years passed, the numerous benefit and social clubs continued that theatrical tradition in labor halls, ethnic centers and in traditional theaters. New York's Hispanic population was primarily peninsular until 1930, and *zarzuelas* such as *Luisa Fernández* and *La del soto del Parral* dominated the stage. Classical repertory was maintained with works such as *La vida es sueño* and *Don Juan Tenorio,* but the typical production was a comedy or a melodrama.

The economic and political circumstances of the 1930s almost destroyed this nascent theatrical tradition; plays opened to virtually empty houses. The Cubans who came to form almost forty percent of the New York population by 1930 were to be joined by Puerto Rican emigrants in the 1940s. Unlike the Spanish, and to a large extent, the Cuban population, the primarily rural Puerto Rican emigrant had no established theatrical tradition. Indeed, James Collins points out the lamentable situation of Puerto Rican theatre:

> During the first four decades of American political domination of the island, there were only two notable works of theatre that hinted at the form Puerto Rican theatre would take in the forties and the fifties. They were the national poet Llorens Torres' *El Grito de Lares* and *Juan Ponce de León* by Carlos Carreras and José Ramírez Santibáñez.[2]

Theatre on the island was limited to the intellectuals and to the urban middle class. Popular art forms for the new arrivals were musical reviews and talking movies.

The musical review continued to dominate the 1940s. Nevertheless, the '40s were not a sterile period. Traditional authors' works continued to be produced, principally los Alvarez Quintero, Arniches, Dicenta and Sardou. Occasionally, new writers and works appeared. Frank Martínez in 1941 produced *De Puerto Rico a New York* in a church hall in the center of El Barrio. However, this play, as well as *La perla de las Antillas* by Jesús Solís and *Nobleza puertorriqueña* by Enrique Codina, failed to attract a public unaccustomed to theatre and attracted to the more readily understood musical review. Hispanic theatre only flourishes in a single sphere—the Barnard-Columbia-Middlebury complex under the leadership of Spanish Civil War refugees, Angel del Río, Amelia Agostini Del Río and of the Cuban political exile, Luis Baralt. The noteworthy contribution of these individuals were the García Lorca productions. Several other theatre groups sprang up, but lasted little time: Rolando Barrera, Dominican actor and his troupe, Futurismo, or Gala, headed by Félix Anteló.

The 1950 to 1965 period can be characterized as the nutritive stage of Hispanic New York theatre. Religious drama, particularly during Lent, is produced by Daniel Morales. Edwin Janer forms La Farándula Panamericana which integrated peninsular works with contemporary Spanish-American, including Puerto Rican, plays. Finally, in 1954, a young director, Roberto Rodríguez, found the vehicle which elicited an overwhelming popular appeal, *La carreta* (The Oxcart) by the then relatively unknown playwright, Réne Marqués. The success of this work united Miriam Colón and Roberto Rodríguez in the Nuevo Círculo Dramático, the company which produced a stable, professional New York Hispanic theatre. Also in 1956, the first play in English treating a Hispanic theme, the *hijo de crianza, Me, Candido,* by Walter Anderson, had a successful run at the Greenwich Mews Theater.

The first half of the 1960s saw many theatrical companies and productions appear and disappear in a weekend. New playwrights appeared—Alvarado, Arriví, Anteló and Rodríguez, among them—as well as a cadre of professional actors and actresses: Miriam Colón, Raúl Julia and Carla Pinza. The year 1964 in which the New York Shakespeare Festival initiated plays in Spanish, and 1965 in which *La carreta* was produced off-Broadway and in which Chelsea Theater presented *Las ventanas* (The windows) of Roberto Rodríguez, music re-entered the theatre, not as in the review, but integrated into *La jíbara,* music by Bobbie Collazo.

The Hispanic theater movement of 1965 to 1977 is composed of three artistic camps, differing in style, purpose, and content. The

The Greenwich Mews production of *La Carretta* in 1954.

La Carreta with Miriam Colón and Raúl Julia in 1965.

first and most established group situated itself within the currents of modern European and American theatre; their productions have been either traditional or experimental. These companies, INTAR, Puerto Rican Traveling Theater, Teatro Repertorio Español and Nuestro Teatro, have a relatively stable physical location and a series of productions in which both actors and directors have formed a sense of "company." They have received the major share of state and federal funds and have established training units for actors, directors and playwrights. Tangential to this group, but with less stability, are such companies as the Centro Cultural Cubano, Duo, Instituto Arte Teatral (INTI), Latin American Theater Ensemble (LATE), Thalia in Queens, and the Tremont Art Group in the Bronx.

These smaller companies are usually led by one or two individuals, for example: Centro Cultural Cubano—Iván Acosta; Duo—Gloria Celaya and Manuel Martínez; IATI—Abdón Villamizar; LATE—Mario Peña; Thalia—Silvia Brito. They are in continuous financial peril.

The second category of Hispanic New York theatre in the period 1965-1977 is the *teatro popular* based on political material which deals with the oppression and with the struggle of the New York Hispanic poor. The audience is challenged to respond to the theatrical circumstances so well known to them. In general, the productions are a collective creation involving actors, writers and sometimes the public. The traditional performance area has been outdoors—the street, the playground, the housing development—,and elements of revolutionary

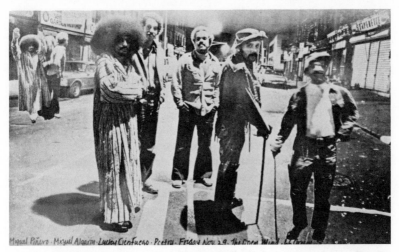

Nuyorican playwrights Lucky Cienfuegos, Miguel Algarín and Miguel Piñero.

street and guerilla theatre merge. Generally, it is leftist proletarian theatre. The leading group in this movement is Teatro 4, a company which uses dance, songs, dialogue and group movement to present sketches of barrio life. Teatro 4 was founded by Oscar Ciccone on the Lower East Side and moved in 1979 to permanent headquarters in El Barrio, the only theater company in Spanish Harlem. Searching the roots of its actors and its audience, it provides a historical dimension and a sociopolitical stance. It represents the essence of agit-prop theater. Similar companies which have appeared and disappeared include Teatro Orilla, Teatro Jurutungo, Teatro Guazábara and El Nuevo Teatro Pobre de América of Pedro Santaliz. Teatro Popular has a political commitment celebrated in its popular festivals held frequently during the summer.

The third division in New York Hispanic theatre between 1965 and 1977 is the New Rican or *Nuyorican* theatre, generally written and produced by a new generation of Puerto Ricans born and raised in the city. The most common organizations were Aquarius, the Latin Insomniacs, El Teatro Ambulante de Bimbo Rivas, the Rican Organization for Self Advancement, Teatro Otra Cosa, The Family and the Nuyorican Poets Cafe. Their working language is the Spanish-English mixture spoken in El Barrio and more noticeably on the Lower East Side (Losaida). Nuyorican writers have typically used the streets, hustling, prostitution, drugs and sex as their thematic material. The Family was born in the Bedford Hill Correctional Facility and has spawned other prison-based groups in various centers on the East Coast. Its workshop also produced the play, *Short Eyes*, by Miguel Piñero, which won the Obie and the New York Drama Critics Award for Best American Play of the 1973-1974 season.

In summary, it can be said that the period 1965-1977 marked the adolescence of Hispanic theatre in New York. A cultural tradition of more than fifty years existed, but the early history is European. An adolescent grows irregularly, in spurts, and is often unbalanced in his development. Hispanic theatre in New York in the first sixty years from 1917 to 1977 had its moments of coordination, clarity and development.

What has happened since 1977 to these three classifications—theater of European tradition, *teatro popular* and Nuyorican theater? Let us examine the trends over the past five years.

Within the three classifications, the stable first group has remained at the forefront and, at times, has become lost and confused in its primacy. The Puerto Rico Traveling Theater, now located in a permanent setting just west of the New York Theater District, had an auspicious season prior to its move. The production of the Colombian work, *I Took Panama*, became a statement favoring Puerto Rican independence. The Tenth Anniversary production of *La Carreta* assembled an all-star cast and became a showcase for Hispanic theatre. However, the startling naturalistic production of *Simpson Street* by the young playwright and actor, Eddie Gallardo, opened to spectators, both in Spanish and English, the world of the South Bronx. *Simpson Street*, called "the pain of captured lives," is the tale of a family and the women who use the household as their living room, an apartment cheaply decorated with plastic slipcovers and tinted religious pictures. The language used in the play integrates the Spanish spoken by the urban Puerto Rican with the New York idiom. This epitome of Hispanic theatre was followed by a lackluster season marked by *Los Soles Truncos* of René Marqués with distinguished Puerto Rican actresses, a deadly *La muerte no entrará en palacio*, and a *Betances* by Jaime Carrero which lumbered onto the stage and slowly sunk into the basement. This current season seems more interesting, if dated: Ruibal's *El hombre y la mosca*, Jacobo Morales' *Aquélla, la otra, este y aquel* and Egon Wolf's *Flores de papel*.

The productions of Morales and Wolf have two-person casts and good directors. They were well performed: professionally with a stern directorial eye (Victoria Espinosa) and careful attention to sets and lighting, an infrequent occurrence. However, the audiences were sparse.

The emphasis is being placed on directorial concepts and young dramatists are not permitted to produce their works. A similar pattern occurs if the productions of INTAR, located on the new 42nd Street Theater Row, are analyzed. The productions are divided into two categories: classical works set in new settings by directorial concepts not often well represented [María Irene Fornés' *La vida es sueño* and Dolores Prida's *Crisp (Los intereses creados)*] and those written with INTAR's founder, Max Ferra. The recent Arrabal production of the *Great Triumph of Jesus Christ, Karl Marx and Shakespeare* was a poorly written, propagandistic farce with a mediocre cast and no visible direction. Others have succeeded: *Carmencita*, the opera set in contemporary New York; *Swallows*, a somewhat melodramatic musical review of Cuban refugees and *Rice and Beans*. Classic repertory has existed with productions of *Los soles truncos*, *Miss Margarita's Way* and *La Dama Duende*. However, more recently, INTAR has decided to present works in English, playing to the more traditional Greenwich Village (Uptown), Theater Row audience.

Little innovation is found in the production of Nuestro Teatro which alternates philosophic plays such as *Las manos de Dios*, *Prohibido suicidarse en Primavera* with *Plaza Suite*, *Mi suegra está loca* and its omnipresent Lorciana: *Yerma*, *La zapatera prodigiosa*, etc. Lorca sells out to school audiences, thus *Bodas de Sangre* and *La casa de Bernarda Alba*, have also been produced by Teatro Repertorio Español, which has traditionally produced a playbill of middle class parlor drama *(Te juro, Juana, que tengo ganas; Los japoneses no esperan* and *La fiaca)* and its omnipresent classic, Spanish peninsular works represented in the language of the period: *La Celestina; Los habladores* y *La dama duende*. This year's season has been marked by *La Corte del Faraón*, an updated *zarzuela* with actors in drag which makes a vain attempt to hold the attention of any slightly serious spectators. Thus, it can be said that the traditional European and Latin American theatre remains the domain of the major Hispanic New York theatres. However, directorial concepts, attempts to have big name authors, a stellar cast, perhaps the ultimate appeal to a broader non-Hispanic audience seems to be the direction of INTAR, PRTR, Nuestro Teatro and Teatro Repertorio Español. Young playwrights such as Mila Conway, María Norman, Víctor Fernández Fragoso, Pedro Pietri and Eddie Gallardo, feel frozen out.

The second rank of traditional theatre is still open to experimentation. Indeed these theatres represent the newer writers, directors and concepts. LATE, under Mario Peña's direction, continues to produce original works, often written by himself. *La Ramera de la Cueva*, *Attapolis* and *El pez que fuma* all involved fantasy and experimentation in language, costuming and direction. Their recent production of René Ariza's *La vuelta a la manzana* was a stunning descent into an absurd world of Arrabal, Beckett and Triana. *Ammo*, in contrast, is a pamphleteering, flat romantic crusade. However, the desire to experiment and to risk failure marks this theatre. The Centro Cultural Cubano which first produced *El super* and which has contributed dramatic works plus readings to the Hispanic New York scene, collapsed in 1979 for financial reasons. The Centro's Iván Acosta and Omar Torres showcased works for the Hispanic community. Its artistic goals and values were noteworthy, but its operating costs were too high.

Herberto Dumé's theatre no longer exists—the loss of a creative

Poster for Acosta's *El Super.*

spirit on the New York stage. Thalia (in Queens) continues to produce the works which a bourgeois audience will appreciate. Silvia Brito has attracted a new audience: the emerging middle class. The productions are professionally orchestrated, directed and performed. Duo Theater, whose female leadership has gone largely without recognition—María Norman, Dolores Prida, Gloria Celaya, Ilka Payán—has produced *Beautiful señoritas* and *Coser y Cantar,* two works by Dolores Prida. Both works by that playwright show the development of a mature creative spirit. Even more recently, the staged readings of Duo, in memory of Víctor Fernández Fragoso, have produced a wealth of work by younger dramatists. Guillermo Gentile's *Con las alas encogidas,* María Mar's stunning portrayal of sex roles and stereotype, *Vice versa,* Omar Torres' Cuban family drama *Dreamland Melody,* Mila Conway's seminal *La Prenda Brenda,* Rubén González's satiric study of bilingualism *Viví Arriba,* as well as Herminio Vargas' *Mucho Macho,* Randy Barceló's *Canciones de la vellonera* and Papo Menéndez's *La Terapia* show that the dramatist's talent is there and active, but only through the staged readings of Duo and by Carla Pinza's Henry Street Settlement House is the public made aware of the new uncharted and unproduced talent. A new presence now emerging in New York is T.O.L.A., based in the Center for Inter-American Relations under the direction of the Argentinian director, Alberto Minero. Its facilities and its strong ties to the Spanish Institute and International Theater provide a new audience and a predisposition to new ideas. Occasionally, a Hispanic work will be staged by a winter series of family-oriented ethnic heritage plays among which, in the winter of 1981, Tato Lavierra's *La Chefa* was produced. This family history, using a dynamic dramatist's technique of bequethal letters, monologues and narrative actions, illustrates the new tendency of a Nuyorican poet who has moved out of the boundaries and constraints of the Poet's Cafe in search of a richer esthetic.

During the adolescent years of 1965-1977, two other tendencies were cited: *teatro popular* and Nuyorican Theater. Both these tendencies have been reduced in number and in influence. *Teatro popular* is still advocated by Teatro 4 under the direction of Oscar Ciccone. Their *Tiempo de amor y guerra,* a collective creation, is touring this season. They continue to produce theatre festivals such as those of 1976 and 1980.

The Third Latin American Popular Theatre Festival (1982) sponsored by Joseph Pappa, Teatro 4 and el Museo del Barrio, was broadened to include more black representation and non-Spanish-speaking groups.

Among the invited groups were Grupo Acto, Argentina; Teatro Experimental de Calí, Colombia; Cubana de Acero, Cuba; Teatro Gratey, Dominican Republic; Teatro Vivo, Guatemala; Colectivo Denuncia,

Mexico; Nixtayolero, Nicaragua; Grupo de Teatro Tablazos, Puerto Rico; Gropo Vrecha, El Salvador; Grupo Rafael Briceño, Venezuela; Teatro de la Esperanza, California; and the Bread and Puppet Theater, Vermont.

From the New York area came Marvin Felix Camillo and the Family, Pregones, the Puerto Rican Traveling Theater, Ntozake Shange and Teatro 4. After the festival, a three-day Congress of Theater Artists was held at el Museo del Barrio. To this writer's knowledge, no other such theatre similar to Teatro 4 and *teatro popular* exists in New York. Teatro Juruntungo has relocated to New Jersey.

Nuyorican theatre seems to be at a standstill. The Nuyorican Poet's Cafe functions as a community center. Readings occur infrequently. Dramatic constructive plays in process are produced. Little maturity is seen. The language and the street scenes represented by the poetry of Piñero, Algarín and Cienfuegos in their 1975 collection now seem vapid and repetitious. The drug-laden texts of Loisaida's *Avenues A, B and C* seem empty and bombastic in the 1980s. Young writers emerge—14-year-old male prostitutes, 15-year-old pregnant ghetto dwellers—but their dramatic laments seem hackneyed and void. Indeed, Miguel Piñero's latest play is once again based on 42nd Street and the young hustlers of Playland, but national recognition has awarded him a Guggenheim for 1982. The Family, which under the leadership of Marvin Felix Camillo was born in prison workshops and has spawned numerous offspring, continues to recruit new dramatists and actors. *Bempires* by Juan Shalum-Alzul was a study of youth gangs. In contrast with Piñero's hustlers, there is a message of hope, albeit wishful thinking.

Therefore, since 1977 the following conclusions can be made. Young, creative playwrights exist and are occasionally produced—for example, Gallardo's *Simpson Street*—but too often their works are limited to staged readings. They are in contact and dialogue constantly and freely about their creations. Hopefully, Mila Conway, María Mar, María Norman, Papo Meléndez, Omar Torres, Randy Barceló, Guillermo Gentile and Eddie Gallardo will find stages for their work. However, it seems highly unlikely that the big four Hispanic theaters, INTPR, PRTT, NY and TRE will produce them. These theaters are insulated in directorial concepts and a search for publicity through major productions of known authors or of distinguished actors and actresses. Some directors have realized their need to expand horizons. René Busch of the Teatro Repertorio Español has been serving this past spring as resident director at the Milwaukee Repertory Theater, preparing a new production in translation of Calderón de la Barca.

Teatro popular, with its revolutionary, guerrilla street audiences, its social causes and its collective conscience, is attracting a limited public, although its presence in the Barrio is recognizable. In a similar manner, the Nuyorican Theater seems to be losing itself in an onanistic rite of linguistic thematic isolation. Only Tato Laviera seems to have escaped from these constraints. The maturity of Hispanic New York Theatre is marked by permanent stages, a ruling elite, and an undercurrent of young writers.

In the second fifty years since that 1917 production of *The Land of Joy,* the possibilities are there. Young writers will lead the way, but they may not always be on the Hispanic stage. They write in English and Spanish. They project universal themes. The rite of passage has to be endured. They collaborate and welcome criticism from fellow dramatists. These individuals will create the Hispanic New York theatre history of the future.

[1] For a more complete analysis of the period prior to 1977, see John Miller, "Hispanic Theatre in New York," *Revista Chicano-Riqueña* 7/1 (Spring 1978), 40-59.

[2] J. A. Collins, *Contemporary Theater in Puerto Rico* (San Juan: Department of Education, Commonwealth of Puerto Rico, 1979), p. 6.

Maida Watson-Espener
Florida International University

Ethnicity and the Hispanic American Stage: The Cuban Experience

Spanish-language theatre is alive and well today in Miami. Both professional and amateur theatrical groups such as Teatro Avante, Bellas Artes, La Comedia, La Danza, Las Máscaras and the Prometeo Players of Miami Dade Community College present Spanish-language plays to Miami's Latin American audiences. And yet, few if any of these plays are written by Hispanics living in the United States. Despite the great amount of prose and poetry[1] written and published by the Cuban exile community, few plays are written by that community and fewer yet are ever staged. The dramatic production of Cuban-American authors exists as a literary theatre, published in occasional magazines, typed and passed from hand to hand. This fact is of particular interest to us when we compare it to the recent, but growing, production of plays by the two other Spanish-speaking minorities in the United States: Chicanos and Puerto Ricans.[2] Why, may we ask, is there such a limited production of original plays?

A final and total answer to this question is beyond the scope of this paper because it must, of necessity, rest on a base of documented, comparative studies of the societies of the three groups. Works of this nature, although badly needed in the field of comparative Hispanic ethnicity, are not yet available. Since the theatre, in contrast to novels, poetry and essays, is a genre which must exist in relation to a community of theatre goers, the necessity of relating literature to society becomes an imperative. Nevertheless, a preliminary inquiry into the nature of Cuban theatre written in the United States can be of use to us in arriving at a better understanding of the phenomena of exile literature and of the differences and similiarities among Cubans, Puerto Ricans and Chicanos in the United States. This paper thus presents an introductory study of the purpose, language, themes and techniques of the plays written by authors of Cuban descent living in the United States during the last twenty years. We will leave for other authors or later studies such equally interesting questions as the relationship of this theatre to the stage in post-revolutionary Cuba and in-depth studies of the individual authors.

A problem of terminology, whether to call this theatre Cuban-American or Cuban theatre in exile, underlines immediately the complexity and diversity of the Cuban experience in the United States. Terms such as Cuban-American theatre and Cuban theatre in exile are directly related to the process of a minority culture's assimilation into United States society or its continued existence as a foreign group living only temporarily in the United States. The term Cuban-American, for example, presupposes the creation of a new culture, one unique to the experience of the Cubans in the United States. The second term, Cuban theatre in exile, on the other hand, emphasizes the maintenance of the pre-exile cultures. Neither term describes completely the writings of authors of such varied background as those included in our study.

The problem is further delineated when we compare the purpose of Chicano and Nuyorican theatre and the connotations of their names. The term Chicano theatre, instead of Mexican-American, for the plays written by Mexican Americans during the last decade, reflects a definite political orientation, the expression of a period of emerging ethnic consciousness. The use of the term Chicano reminds us that the historical roots of Mexican American theatre's most recent renaissance are found in the Delano strike and Luis Valdez's Teatro Campesino. Puerto Rican theatre in the United States has largely manifested itself as part of the experimental and political theatre in New York City and as the external reflection of developing Puerto Rican consciousness in New York. Thus Nuyorican theatre, a mixture of the words New York and Puerto Rico, exemplifies the characteristics of this theatre: a popular theatre produced by Puerto Ricans, many of whom are second-generation Puerto Ricans, written with the clear purpose of inspiring a change in society's treatment of their people.

The writings of the Cuban authors that we will examine in this paper are not the products of any such unified political and social movements. They are members of a group which evidences a high degree of assimilation to the dominant Anglo-Saxon society and which is characterized at the same time by a great degree of variety within this group. Cuban psychologist Fernando González-Reigosa believes that Cubans may be more varied than other ethnic groups because, contrary to popular misconception, the Cuban exile included not just the middle classes but a total society.[3] Antonio Jorge and Raúl Moncarz support this belief in the range of social classes within the exile community.[4]

González Reigosa's research is of particular value to us in dealing with literary nomenclature. His groupings of the Cuban community are based on two variables: the degree of assimilation to the dominant culture and varying socio-economical and educational realities. Among his four groups he lists what he calls the frozen culture, that is, the culture of those who arrived in the United States with a fully developed set of cultural patterns and who reflect "the idealized values of the Cuban culture before 1959, that is, idealized because in many cases we have created a mythology of how we were in Cuba and what Cuba was like."[5] A theater that would reflect the aspirations of this group would by necessity be called "Cuban theater in exile." González-Reigosa also describes the development of what he believes will be a new culture, one uniquely both urban and North American, which he calls "Cubish" and defines as a group that "refuses to lose its Hispanic values, but feels comfortable dealing with problems of this country and society."[6] This group, if it has a theatrical expression, could be called Cuban-American theater.

It is the first group, Cuban exile theater, that predominates among the playwrights we will examine here. Cuban-American theater includes only one playwright, Omar Torres. Of the eight playwrights—Julio Matas, José Cid Pérez, Leopoldo Hernández, José Sánchez-Boudy, Celedonio González, Raúl de Cárdenas, Matías Montes-Huidobro and Omar Torres, whose work we will survey in this study—only one, Omar Torres, was born after 1935. The details of their exile vary from one dramatist to another, but one thing is clear: they arrived in the United States with a fully developed set of cultural patterns, fulfilling one of González Reigosa's definitions of those who form part of the "frozen culture." They bring with them a definite literary heritage and, in many cases, previous experience as actors or writers.

Their decrease in dramatic production after the first years of exile further corroborates their existence as a group isolated from their exile surroundings. Among the seven playwrights who form the writers of Cuban theatre, only Celedonio González and José Sánchez-Boudy have produced more than an occasional play since their arrival in the United States. This lack of an abundant literary production reinforces our belief that drama, unlike poetry and prose, is the result of an active theatre movement. The plays that were written in Cuba by most of these authors were a result of the development of experimental theatre in pre-Castro Cuba. When that Spanish-speaking public disappeared as a result of exile to a non-Spanish speaking country, the writing of plays also decreased.

The individualistic nature of the Cuban community in the United States is mirrored in the personal and aesthetic purpose of their writings. Only Omar Torres has a social purpose akin to that of Chicano and Puerto Rican writers. Torres states that the purpose of his theatre is to "present a reality with which the Latin American or Hispanic man can identify and through which he can anlayze himself."[7] But the function of theatre as a means to portray reality, a time honored purpose, is interpreted by other writers as a personal, psychological reality. José Sánchez-Boudy states that "theatre mirrors life," and he immediately adds his definition of life by saying "reality is varied, both exterior and interior. Theatre does not have a social purpose, it only serves to mirror this reality."[8] Raúl de Cárdenas answers when asked the purpose of his theatre, "I write because I want to say something and say it without moralizing; I just want to express something personal, and since I don't paint, nor sing, well then, I write."[9]

The themes of Cuban exile theatre both continue tendencies in pre-Castro Cuban theatre and duplicate developments in current literary genres. In pre-1959 Cuba, two kinds of plays reflected a subjective approach to reality: psychological plays and absurd plays, the former outnumbering the latter.[10] The theatre of Cubans in the United States continues this interest in psychological rather than social realities developed initially in Cuba. After the Cuban Revolution two trends were evidenced in island dramatic works: one for essentially realistic, revolutionary plays and one for plays in which "the dramatic preoccupation with reflecting a collectively recognizable social reality is replaced by a desire to theorize on the ideological meaning of the Revolution."[11] Cuban exile theatre mirrors this desire to theorize about the basic problems of man's nature rather than deal with specific social problems.

Four subjects predominate in the writings of the exiles: the psychological isolation of exile life, the rise of the newly-rich and their relationship to the Cuban community, pre-Castro Cuba and man's inhumanity to man. Escape themes predominate among the Cuban exile writers, perhaps as an expression of the isolation and alienation of exile life. In José Cid's *La última conquista*, the solitude and isolation of an old Don Juan represents the feeling of a man who has lost his country. The characters are upper class types: Pedro, the rich Don Juan, and Mariana, the strong, noble woman who represents the patriotic ideals that do not seem real to this life any more. Their empty life and lack of communication are universal themes as well as outward representations of the emotional tone of exile. Pedro's final effort to seduce Mariana is followed by a sense of loss; it is "la última conquista" (the last seduction), the impossible final attempt to regain the motherland.

In Julio Mata's play *Penelope Inside Out*, one of the few plays of the exile writers written in English, symbolic characters identified only as The Man and The Woman experience the same sense of emptiness and isolation. An abandoned woman reencounters her old husband who abandons her again. In Leopoldo Hernández' *Cuatro de julio*, the theme of lack of communication appears during the conversations of a couple celebrating twenty years of married life. Likewise, in Omar

Torres' *En el tronco de un árbol,* a couple celebrates its 25th wedding anniversary, but experiences problems in communication. Words and phrases are repeated over and over to emphasize the sameness of the situation. The title of the play is the name of a song that they both liked at one time, but now only one remembers. They avoid all matters that involve direct communication; the words, "Bueno, vamos a dejar eso a un lado" are repeated over and over again.

Lack of communication mirrors the exile's feeling of being cut off, both from the past and from the present. Lack of knowledge of English, the creation of a protective microcosm through Cuban TV, radio and neighborhoods, and the political barriers imposed by the Castro regime all reinforce the feeling of being rootless. The exile's son, Betico, in Omar Torres' *If You Dance the Rumba* puts this feeling into words, as he says to his father, "You have roots, we have nothing, Nena and I are all the kids of my age. We don't belong here, we don't belong there, we don't belong anywhere. We're floating. We're not Cubans, we're not Americans, we're nothing."[12]

Language plays an important function in creating this feeling of isolation. The character of José in Celedonio González' *José Pérez, candidato a la alcaldía* says, "I live with the eternal dream of returning some day to Manguito. Of being again in my country and being able to feel again a man all the time. And not to be afraid that someone will talk to me and I will not be able to answer them."[13] In the play, *El Super,* by Iván Acosta, Roberto the "super" in a New York apartment building cannot talk to the Building Inspector. He escapes from the problem of language by listening to Spanish radio and TV. Iris Chacón, a popular Puerto Rican TV personality, becomes a recurring symbol in the play, a protective mother-sex object who warms him from the physical and psychological cold of the New York winters.

Language becomes also an outward sign of the Cuban's rejection by the Anglo world. José Pérez in *José Pérez, candidato a la alcaldia,* discusses the fact that Dade County is a bilingual county. He voices his fears that he might be at a disadvantage because he cannot speak English. His wife Emilia says, "Este es un Condado Bilingüe," but José Pérez answers, "Sí, pero los americanos no son más que una lengua."[14]

The exiles are also divided among themselves by different degrees of assimiliation. The theme of Castro serves as a dividing line between those who have adapted more to the new life and those who still reject it. Aurora in José Sánchez-Boudy's play, *La Soledad de la playa larga,* expresses the feeling of those who have not assimilated and feel cut off from their roots. Referring to the forced departure from Cuba, she says "They will put up a wall between you and your country, and between those who stay and who leave."[15] Juan adds later on in the play, "Because to live in a foreign country is not to live. It is to be dead, always dead."[16]

An important escape mechanism to deal with the isolation of the present is the idealization and nostalgia for the past. As in the exile prose, there is a special predilection for what Seymour Menton has called "the portrayal of prerevolutionary Cuba and particularly prerevolutionary Havana."[17] It is this phenomenon that González-Reigosa refers to when he describes the frozen generation. In Omar Torres' *If You Dance the Rumba,* one of the characters states, "We, we're living facing backwards. Always looking backwards because we need to live our memories to be able to live, to be able to face all this."[18]

Omar Torres develops the theme of nostalgia further in another of his plays, *Dreamland Melody,* written entirely in English. The play takes place in a small Cuban town during a revolution and five years later in Miami. Dreams play a pivotal role in the stage action. Peter, the main character, has been living in a dreamland shadow and he and the others talk about dreams, the numbers they deduce from them for the lottery, and their lives which seem to form part of the same dreams. Another of the characters, William, wants only to listen to his music and escape. He doesn't want change and represents the lack of change in the Cuban exile frozen generation.

During the exile experience, nostalgia for Cuba becomes gradually displaced to nostalgia for the new Cuba Mecca, Miami. In *El Super,* the characters talk during the play about moving to Miami and escaping the cold of New York. Roberto and Aurelia are frozen both culturally, to use González-Reigosas' term, and physically, as they seek to escape from the difficult winters of New York. Through their friends they desperately try to maintain their former Cuban life in the Big Apple. Roberto's responsibility for keeping the furnace in the apartment building stocked becomes a symbol of his attempt to ward off the cold of life in exile. Everytime the furnace breaks down he is reminded through the tenants' insults of his menial and unfulfilled life. In contrast, Miami seems to him a fantasy of sun, warmth and palm trees. The movie version of the play carried this symbol even further. On the screen, the snow and the furnace become intense reminders of this conflict between two opposing forces: cold/heat, New York/Miami, exile life/Cuba.

Another theme that appears frequently in the writings of Cuban exiles is man's inhumanity to man. A thinly disguised Fidel Castro dominates the plays of two writers, Matías Montes Huidobro and José Sánchez-Boudy. In Montes Huidobro's *Ojos para no ver,* published in the early years of exile, a beast-like character identified only as El Comandante stalks the stage condemning everyone who opposes him to the shooting squad. His tactics are to kill all others in order not to be killed, destroy in order to avoid self-destruction. He states his philosophy when he says, "Y si corto, ¿por qué voy a temer ser cortado? ¿No es la castración . . . de los otros, la seguridad de mis testículos?"[19] Sánchez-

The Screen: 'El Super,' A Cuban-American Tale

By VINCENT CANBY

For the last 10 of his 42 years, Roberto, a former bus driver in Havana, has been living in New York exile with his wife, Aurelia, and their 17-year-old daughter, Aurelita. Roberto not only suffers the life of an outsider, he embraces it as well as the isolation, the humiliation and the homesickness that go with it. Because he refuses to learn English, the best he can do by way of employment is a job as superintendent in a large tenement on the Upper West Side.

"El Super," a Cuban-American feature film shot in New York, opens early on a Sunday morning in February as Roberto tries to sleep while angry tenants upstairs bang on the pipes demanding that the boiler be turned on. They are entitled, but he has forgotten. Finally he rouses himself. Says Aurelia of the commotion, "I can't stand English the first thing in the morning."

A little later, Aurelia surveys their neat basement apartment, furnished with all of the necessities, including a television set and an electric blender, and reports that she's tired of peering out the window and seeing nothing but people's feet. "It's like looking at the world from underneath," which is pretty much the way Roberto sees things.

From this beginning you might suspect that "El Super" would be grim, but you'd be wrong. It's a funny, even-tempered, unsentimental drama about people in particular transit. Roberto thinks of his life as being a sort of long, boring, nonstop flight from Cuba that will eventually circle back there, while Aurelita and a number of their friends are losing no time in assimilating.

The film, the first feature to be co-directed by Leon Ichaso and Orlando Jimenez-Leal, is based on Ivan Acosta's play of the same name that was produced originally by the Cuban Cultural Center in New York in 1977. It will be presented in the New Directors/New Films series at the Museum of Modern Art today at 6 P.M. and Wednesday at 8:30 P.M. It is scheduled to have its commercial opening in New York in June.

The Cast

EL SUPER, directed by Leon Ichaso and Orlando Jimenez-Leal; produced and adapted for the screen (in Spanish with English subtitles) by Manuel Arce and Mr. Ichaso, based on the original play "El Super" by Ivan Acosta; camera, Mr. Jimenez-Leal; edited by Gloria Piñeyro; music by Enrique Ubieta. At the New Directors/New Films series, Museum of Modern Art, 53d Street west of Fifth Avenue. Running time: 90 minutes.

Roberto	Raymundo Hidalgo-Gato
Aurelia	Zully Montero
Pancho	Reynaldo Medina
Aurelita	Elizabeth Peña
Cuco	Juan Granda
La China	Hilda Lee
Inspector	Phil Joint
Predicador	Leonardo Soriano
Bobby	Efrain López-Neri
Ofelia	Ana Margarita Martinez-Casado

"El Super" is not an especially political film, though it is concerned with working-class people who fled the revolution. Its most uninhibitedly comic character is a manic fellow named Pancho, a veteran of the Bay of Pigs fiasco, who is rabidly anti-Castro and everywhere sees Communist conspirators, including the loony man who pushes into Roberto's apartment one Sunday afternoon to preach Christ's Gospel.

"El Super" is much less about politics than it is about the disorientation of exiles who become living metaphors for the human condition. Such a person is Roberto, played with infinite good humor and common sense by Raymundo Hidalgo-Gato. The role, like the screenplay by Manuel Arce and Mr. Ichaso, is extremely well written as it avoids the usual impulse of such realistic drama to state in large, long speeches what it intends to be about. "El Super" works entirely within its characters and events.

The film was obviously produced on a very low budget, but with care, intelligence and with a cast of marvelous Cuban and Puerto Rican actors. In

Raymundo Hidalgo-Gato

addition to Mr. Hidalgo-Gato, they include Zully Montero as Aurelia, Reynaldo Medina as Pancho, and Elizabeth Piña as Aurelita.

NY Times review of *El Super*.

Boudy places his merciless tyrant in the Puritan New England colonies as an unbending relentless elder. A character named McIver represents the opposition to Castro. In a playlet entitled *El hombre de ayer y de hoy,* McIver is killed because he attempts to combat tyranny.

In other Sánchez-Boudy plays, the author enlarges his focus from the specific problem of a tyrant's repression to an examination of the reasons for man's inhumanity to man. One possible explanation seems to be man's own nature. In *La cuidad de humanitas,* Sánchez-Boudy says "Los hombres tienen los gusanos dentro y salen por todos lados. Los hombres son una gusanera."[20] In this playlet, a character named Humanidad looks for the office of the Social Security Funeral Parlor and is ignored and attacked by everyone she meets. In other plays, the author continues this theme. In *El negro con color a azufre,* set in the pre-Civil War South, a man decides to free his slaves and faces death threats, not only from the other white planters, but from the slaves themselves. In *Los asesinos, los asesinos,* a man runs through New York pursued by unknown murderers. At first he believes that the murderers are the city of New York itself; finally at the end we see that it is his own background, his family, schooling, etc. Man is destroyed, finally, by the forces within him instead of anything else.

Cuban exile theatre reflects a variety of techniques, ranging from the continuation of the ever-popular theatre of the absurd, to the use of traditional theatrical realism and the adoption of the comic devices and characterization used in the Cuban popular stage, "el teatro bufo." Orlando Rodríguez Sardiñas' playlet, *La Visita,* is an example of the popularity of theatre of the absurd. Through the skillful use of repetition, satirization of clichés and doble characters, the author underlines the absurdity of the life led by two old maids who live waiting for the perfect man to arrive. When the visit finally takes place, they eat the visitor and are by this means finally able to totally own him.

Interestingly, Cuban-exile theatre does not utilize many of the techniques of the experimental drama of the '60s and '70s such as agit-prop theatre, living theatre and collective creation. Perhaps because of the assocation of some of the vanguard groups with the political left, they have been largely ignored by the exile writers. Another reason could be found in the fact that Cuban exile theatre has its roots in the theatrical movements of the '50s in Cuba and Western Europe, a time dominated by the Post World War II predilection for the absurd. In contrast, Chicano theatre begins with Luis Valdez' Teatro Campesino, which borrowed heavily from the San Francisco mime troop and agit-prop. Current Chicano theatre groups have continued their involvement with experimental theatre through workshops in collective creation and seminars with Enrique Buenaventura, among other Latin American avant-guarde dramatists. Nuyorican theatre experiences a similar development.

Carmen Montejo, first lady of the Cuban stage.

The elaborate costuming of a Miami production of *Don Juan Tenorio*.

It begins in association with off-Broadway experimental groups and continues to develop through close ties with the descendants of the vanguard movements.

During the last few years, the Cuban exile stage has experienced a change, both in content and intensity. In pre-Revolutionary Cuba, two forms of theatre predominated: popular theatre, consisting mainly of vaudeville and "bufo" theatre,[21] and a more intellectual theatre whose repertoire consisted of adaptations of Spanish, European and North American plays. During the first two decades of exile, Cubans were treated to a repertoire of vaudeville and light comedy. Current events and political subjects are largely ignored and plays of a more intellectual or artistic nature usually closed after a few performances.

Since the Mariel boat-lift, though, several small theatres have sprung up in Miami, many staffed by actors who themselves arrived just recently from Cuba. These theatres stage plays of both a popular kind and a more serious nature and play in many cases to audiences who have never been to live theatre before. Using characters borrowed from Cuban popular radio shows and the *teatro "bufo"* they deal with current events, both in Cuban and Miami. The familiar types, such as Mamacusa (the old maid), Prematura and Trespatines, are joined by new characters, Fidel and his brother Raúl Resbaloso. Plays with titles like *Me voy para Cuba, fuá,* which deal with the problems faced by refugees when they travel to Cuba to visit their family, and *A Vicente le llegó un pariente,* which tells the story of Vicente's cousin from Cuba who arrived on the Mariel boat-lift, combine the technique of the old vaudeville with references to a new life.

Theatres such as Teatro Avante continue the pre-Revolutionary interest in a more serious and intellectual stage. Avante's directors, Eduardo Corbé and Mario Ernesto Sánchez, have directed during the last two years *Aire Frío* by the Cuban playwright Virgilio Piñera and *Las niñas ricas de Camagüey* (The Rich girls of Camaguey), a Cubanized treatment of García Lorca's *The House of Bernarda Alba*. Miguel González Pando *(La Familia Pilón)* and Rafael Blanco *(Marielitos)* have demonstrated promise as playwrights.

Whatever may be the aesthetic value of these plays, one thing is clear: a modest sized theatre-going public is finally being created for the first time in Miami. From this surge in dramatic activity with its interest in satire and contemporary events may very well come the seeds of the new Cuban-American drama. The stylized, symbolic figure of Fidel has metamorphosed and is now the stock, comic figure of "Se le fue por el Mariel hasta el santero de Fidel." From Fidel to Mariel, Cuban-exile theatre completes its cycle of development and initiates what may be a new artistic expression of a new culture, Cuban-American.

[1] For information regarding prose work produced by Cuban exiles see: Solomon Lipp, "The Anti-Castro Novel," *Hispania*, 58 (May 1975), pp. 284-296; Seymour Menton, *Prose Fiction of the Cuban Revolution* (Austin: University of Texas Press, 1976); José Sánchez-Boudy, *Historia de la literatura cubana en el exilo* (Miami: Universal, 1975); Antón A. Fernández Vásquez, *La Novelística Cubana de la Revolución* (Miami: Universal, 1979). For information regarding poetry written by Cuban exiles see: Ana Rosa Nuñez, *Poesía en Exodo* (Miami: Universal, 1969).

[2] For information regarding the theatre of Mexican-Americans and Puerto Ricans living in the United States see: John C. Miller, *Revista Chicano-Riqueña* 6/2 (Invierno, 1978); Pablo Figueroa *Teatro: Hispanic Theatre in New York City 1920-1976* (New York: El Museo del Barrio, 1977) and the numerous publications of Nicolás Kanellos and Jorge Huerta, among which are: Nicolás Kanellos and Jorge Huerta, ed., *Nuevos Pasos: Chicano and Puerto Rican Drama* in *Revista Chicano Riqueña* 7/1 (1979) and *Mexican American Theatre, Then and Now* ed. Nicolás Kanellos (Arte Publico Press, 1983).

[3] Fernando González-Reigosa, "Las culturas del exilo," *Boletín del Instituto de Estudios Cubanos*, Madrid, Spain, October, 1976, p. 1.

[4] Antonio Jorge and Raúl Moncarz, "International Factor Movement and Complementarity: Growth and Entrepreneurship Under Conditions of Cultural Variation," *Research Group for European Migration Problems Bulletin*, Supplement 14 (September 1981), p. 12.

[5] González-Reigosa, p. 1. The translations are mine.

[6] *Ibid.*, p. 11.

[7] Omar Torres, Interview with Cristina Tamargo, *Réplica* 1973, p. 75.

[8] Interview with José Sánchez-Boudy, May 1977, Miami, Florida.

[9] Interview with Raúl de Cárdenas, Miami, Florida, Sept. 24, 1976.

[10] Terry L. Palls, *The Theater in Revolutionary Cuba, 1959-1969*, Unpublished Ph.D. dissertation, Kansas 1974, p. 156.

[11] *Ibid.*, p. 2.

[12] Omar Torres, *If You Dance the Rumba*, unpublished manuscript, no date, p. 39.

[13] Celedonio González, *José Peréz, candidato a la alcaldía*, unpublished manuscript, 1974, p. 48.

[14] *Ibid.*, p. 56.

[15] José Sánchez-Boudy, *La Soledad de la playa larga* (Miami: Universal, 1974), p. 45.

[16] *Ibid.*, p. 73.

[17] Seymour Menton, *Prose Fiction of the Cuban Revolution* (Austin: University of Texas Press, 1976), p. 275.

[18] Omar Torres, *If You Dance the Rumba*, p. 40.

[19] Matías Montes Huidobro, *Ojos para no ver*, unpublished manuscript, p. 43. My translation of this quote is: "and if I cut, then why fear being cut by others? Is not the castration of others, the security of my testicles?"

[20] José Sánchez-Boudy, "La ciudad de Humanitas," *Homo Sapiens*, (Miami: Universal, 1971), p. 71.

[21] Matías Montes Huidobro, *Persona, vida y máscara en el teatro cubano* (Miami: Universal, 1973) pp. 69-71.

Tomás Ybarra-Frausto
Stanford University

I Can Still Hear the Applause.
La Farándula Chicana: Carpas y Tandas de Variedad

Serious theatre can provide a sublime form of aesthetic experience, yet the human spirit is also enriched by those dramatic *genres* that are light and frivolous, full of sparkling wit, music and mirth. The comic idiom incites a smile at human foibles and laughter at the droll relativity of human experience.

Within Mexicano/Chicano communities, humor has been an indispensable companion of endurance. Constant confrontations with the most depressing realities have allowed the Chicano to poke fun at adversity, to ridicule and laugh at his own social condition and thus to spiritually surmount his circumstance. *(No se agüite compadre, ¡es puro pedo!)* The same bawdy, irreverent and satiric sensibility defines the world of the *farándula* and its diverse presentational forms like the *carpas, maromas* and the *teatro de revista y variedades*.[1]

Las Carpas

By the turn of the century, as the region along the Mexican border was developed into an agricultural oasis through the use of Chicano labor and technical skills, itinerant troupes of *carpas* and *maromas* made yearly visits to the *pueblitos* and the *barriadas* of the cities. The following transcriptions from oral history project their ambiance:

La tradición de la carpa se debe ver en el modo de vivir de lo rufiano. Era un modo de entretenimiento para la plebe. Tres tandas diarias, los niños a peseta, adultos a tostón. Allá por los años treintas me acuerdo muy claramente de la Carpa Monsiváis. Yo vivía en Mission, Texas y esta carpa venía através del Valle, tal vez se originaba en San Antonio, Texas. Llegaba a los pueblitos y levantaban su carpa en un solar vacante.

La función empezaba con un intercambio de chistes entre un payaso y una señorita. Había muchas insinuaciones y groserías. Después había una serie de dramas, generalmente trataban cosas trágicas como el tema del amor. El lenguaje de estos sainetes era muy formal y correcto.

Entonces se ponían una serie de canciones para requebrantar. Eran canciones topicales que hablaban de lo que transcurría en ese tiempo. (La orquesta que siempre venía con la carpa era de pito, tambora, cornetín y batería.)

Después que se iban del pueblo, todos nosotros los chamacos tratábamos de imitar lo que habíamos visto. Poníamos nuestras propias funciones para la vecindad y eran muy divertidas. . . .[2]

The *carpa* tradition bonded the spectators and the spectacle in a nexus of social interaction. *Corridistas* sang of traditional heroes and historical events while *declamadores* kept alive the stylized forms of *buen hablar* already assimilated into working class consciousness through the high rhetoric of *Cinco de Mayo* and *Diesiséis de Septiembre* traditions of public speaking. A sentimental library canon was maintained through intense dramatic readings of *poesía de tono menor*. Perennial favorites included "El brindis del bohemio" by Guillermo Aguirre y Fierro and "El Cristo de mi Cabecera" by Rubén C. Navarro. The repertoire of many *declamadores* also included the poetry of Antonio Plaza and Juan de Dios Peza.

Yet the overlay of literary respectability was subverted by the insolent and aggressive spirit of *picardía* based on sexual and political allusions that informed the *carpa* sketches. As the poet Raúl Salinas recalls:

La carpa venía a los pueblitos en el tiempo de frío. Durante el calor estaban en las ciudades grandes. Nunca necesitaban publicidad. Nomás se oían los chismes de que hay venía la carpa maldita y todos los padres de la iglesia decían que no era propio dejar ir a los niños a esas diversiones. Ni tampoco era apropiada para los adultos porque daban mal ejemplo. Las carpas eran para la pura raspa . . . la plebe.

Yo me acuerdo de La Carpa Cubana allá por los años treinta y nueve o cuarenta en Austin, Texas. Allí llegaba la carpa al East Side, a las orillas del traque que era más colonia que *barrio*. La carpa se ponía en un solar vacante entre las calles Cinco y Santa Rosa en el barrio de Buena Vista.

Tenían orquesta que tocaba ritmos tropicales. El animador era un cantante famoso que le decían *El Cáscara*. También venía un payaso llamado *Pina Bora* (Peanut Butter), que se dedicaba a entretener a los niños. *Macaco*, otro cómico lo hacía de "top banana" siguiendo mujeres y haciendo gestos obscenos. Era caso de puros chistes colorados. Después *la vedette* bailaba con unos espejos flashing to the men in the crowd. "Qué le echó la luz a Don Macrino, mira 'amá cómo le echó la luz a Don Chon" . . .

El programa era algo así: Primero salían en escena el payaso y la *vedette* diciendo y actuando una serie de bromas, chistes y relajos:

El payaso: (a la bailarina) Mira qué mona, le pegó la fiebre y se quedó pelona.
El público: ora . . .
El payaso: A ver, miren, miren a Joaquín con su cara de violín.
El publico: ora . . . te sales . . .

Después todo se volvía albures, puro pedo. Luego que se apaciguaba el público, ponían un drama. Era corto, formal y lagrimoso. Para terminar, venían las maromas—por ejemplo, ponían un tubo de unos cincuenta pies de alto y se subía este señor y hacia suertes . . .[3]

Rooted in such popular traditions as the circus, village-fair entertainments and non-verbal forms of theatre like the carnival and *mimus* of antiquity, the *carpas* presented spectacles combining dancing, singing and acrobatics. Performance strategies were anchored on the broadly realistic representations of character types in semi-improvised, spontaneous clowning situations. A bawdy irreverent and satiric spirit prevailed. *Carpa* performances were fluid, open, semi-structured presentational events with direct audience interaction and feedback.

From the turn of the century until the late 1940s, *carpas* were a widespread and durable form of entertainment throughout the Southwest. Troupes were often small, extended family-based units performing under canvas in remote rural areas and venturing into the outer boundaries of urban *barrios*.

Rolling into town in rickety worn-out trucks, loaded down with baggage and show paraphernalia, the raggle-taggle troupes hired able-bodied men from the community to help set up their tent in whatever vacant lot was available. After raising the tent, the first order of business prior to a performance was the *convite* (an oral invitation to the show). In retrospect, this preliminary procedure is vividly recalled by a contemporary informant:

"Los chamacos de toda la barriada nos juntábamos como a las cinco o las cinco y media de la tarde el día de la función. Llegaba Reymundo García (de la Carpa García) quien tenía un gran talento para pintarnos de payaso.

Nos pintaba y nos montaba en la plataforma de la troca, una troca vieja y roja. Llevábamos una bocina de esas antiguas como un cono. Esta era el convite que paseaba por las calles de la barriada pitando, gritando y haciendo gran traquilada—¡VENGAN A LA CARPA GARCIA! . . . GRAN FUNCION . . . ¡VENGAN TODOS. . . !

Así el convite con su gritería daba su ronda por diez bloques alrededor, para convidar a toda la gente. Y a la funcion venía gente de tan retirado como dos o tres millas de donde era la presentación."[4]

Carpa performances featured an eclectic mixture of acrobatics, clowning, pantomime, comedic turns, dramatic monologues, singing and dancing.

La Carpa García,[5] a famous family-based troupe from San Antonio, Texas, performed throughout the Southwest from 1914 until the late 1940s. In format, their productions typify the loosely orchestrated, fluid, presentational events centered on the comic and the laughable, that define the *carpa* form:

. . . "Bueno, como yo recuerdo, una función típica tenía las siguientes partes: Empezaba todo con la banda y las luces en el escenario. (Era una máquina que aventaba chispas de luz de diferentes colores ya que la luz se filtraba con papel de celofán.) Por un gran rato tocaba la banda mientras se lucían los *spotlights* de diferentes colores en el escenario. La banda estaba abajo en la tierra o mejor dicho en el aserín.

Luego salía el maestro de ceremonias dando la bienvenida y animando al público con algunos chistes. Después una cantante seguida por un número bailable y un *sketch* cómico.

A mediación de la función prendían las luces y ya estaba instalado un cable sobre el cual Pilar García hacia diferentes suertes. Ella iba vestida de charro. Era fantástica y hasta echaba maromas en el cable. ¡Deslumbraba a todos! Luego salían maromeros y era lo último antes del intermedio.

Ya después comenzaba la banda y otra vez las luces bailando en el escenario. A veces ponían un número de magia. Seguía un intermedio cómico con alguien como El Conqueno, un famoso actor cómico. Hasta podía haber un acto de un contorsionista.

La función siempre terminaba con una *production number* con varias parejas en escena, bailando el jarabe tapatío por ejemplo."[6]

Saturated with a popular ethos, *carpa* productions were freed from a unity of style. While anchored in circus traditions of clowning and acrobatics, performers used whatever presentational form was required to maintain an overall spirit of festivity and frolic. Knockabout action and improvisation were foregrounded, especially in the brief comedic sketches. *Carpas* were an incipient form of what Peter Brook labels the rough theatre:

In the luxury of the high-class theatre, everything can be all of a piece: in a rough theatre a bucket will be banged for a battle, flour used to show faces white with fear. The arsenal is limitless: the aside, the placard, the topical reference, the local jokes, the exploiting of accidents, the songs, the dances, the tempo, the noise, the relying on contrasts, the shorthand of exaggeration, the false noses, the stock types, the stuffed bellies. The popular theatre, freed of unity of style, actually speaks a very sophisticated and stylish language.[7]

The eloquence and vitality of the *carpa's* presentational vocabulary emerged from a mode of heightened intensity in the interaction of performers and audience. Productions gained strength, integrity and coherence through this fluid participatory context.

Oral expression is a pervasive and significant aspect of Chicano culture. In the *cábula* of street corner rapping, the hyperbolic rhetoric of public speaking and the mannered theatrics of *professional declamadores*, the Chicano community affirms and validates a long-standing tradition of *buen hablar*. Within the group, it is a privilege to be recognized as *una persona que sabe hablar*. The approbation generally connotes that the person in question is not merely verbally adequate, but also embellishes everyday speech in aesthetically pleasing ways. Usually such an

Don Fito, the *peladito* of the Carpa García.

Carpa García chorus girls.

individual weaves a varied repertoire of proverbs, anecdotes, jokes and other forms of speech-play into everyday discourse. El *buen hablar* is an important element of being a person who is *bien educada*. By contrast, an individual who might have formal education but lacks an understanding of community-validated norms of behavior, manners and other social codes, can only be called *instruido*. This distinction between *educación* and *instrucción* is rooted in linguistics as well as patterns of self-presentation.

Laughter stimulated by verbal dexterity forms a root source of *carpa* comedic style. Directly linked to the *picardía* of spoken language, much humor stems from adroit manipulations of linguistic resources such as solecisms, malapropisms, turns of phrases and double entendres. *Albures*, an abrasive barrage of wisecracks with sexual allusions and connotations became common stock for *carpa* comedians. A famous exponent of this sort of linguistic virtuosity was the great Mexican comedienne Celia Tejeda. In the *carpas* she was a famous headliner as a *vedette* (a soloist combination of singer, dancer and actress). In the midst of her scintillating performance she would suddenly stop:

> "de pronto se transformaba y cambiaba la expresión y el modo de su figura toda; de amante apasionada pasaba a ser una mujerona lépera de barrio, campeona del calambur gracias a su prodigiosa agilidad mental: durante quince, veinte minutos, cambiaba frases de doble—y a veces de triple—sentido, con los eufóricos espectadores que desataban la lengua para ir construyendo con las respuestas de Celia, un monumento auténtico, eso sí, a la picardía mexicana."[8]

Verbal gamesmanship, criss-crossing the footlights and audience, fused into brief, episodic comic sketches that became core components in *carpa* performances. The *sketch cómico* incorporated type characterizations, mimic acting, slapstick and droll business developed in a rough-and-tumble framework of vernacular dialogues. Varying from short acted-out jokes and anecdotes to more developed compositions sustaining a plotline, the *sketch cómico* gave license to diverse forms of comic mayhem.

The crude and ribald content of many such comic sketches centered around what Mikhail Bakhtin calls "the lower stratum,"[9] humor related to body functions: copulation, birth, growth, eating and defecation. A brief *sketch cómico* from the repertoire of La Carpa García in San Antonio, Texas, sets the tone:

El Cazador

(two compadres meet after a long absence)

1: Orale, compadre, qué gusto en verlo, dichosos los ojos. Pero, a ver, dígame, ¿ónde andaba que no lo he visto por aquí?

2: Ah, compadre, pues fíjese que yo andaba en Africa, cazando leones. Imagínese Ud., yo allá tan lejos metido en la jungla . . . y de repente que me sale un león—uno de esos grandotes! . . . y riata . . . que me lo echo con la carabina! Y de repente, que me sale otro león, y éste era más grande . . . y ya no tenía parque . . .

1: ¿Pues entonces qué pasó, compadre? ¿Qué hizo?

2: ¡Fíjese nomás, que sale un LEON ENORME y brincaba y se revolteaba enseñándome sus dientes! ¡Y luego hasta se resbala, PUM! Pero se levanta con más ganas, gruñendo así muy feo . . . como queriéndome comer.

1: Híjole compadre, ¡pues yo me hubiera zurrado!

2: Ay, compadre, ¿pos por qué cree que se estaba resbalando el león?

The crudity of *carpa* humor often underscored sordid social realities in the Southwest. A dominant theme was the process of *agringamiento* with many sketches lampooning selected aspects of the dominant culture:

1: Oiga, compadre, . . . ¿Ud. habla bien el inglés?

2: No, pos es muy difícil, fíjese nomás, el inglés se lleva mucha saliva.

1: Entonces, mire, ya como tengo la cara.

2: ¡Ah pues, entonces, Ud. ha de ser bueno p'al inglés compadre!

Many asides poked fun at those who attempted to join the melting pot:

"No, si mi compadre ya es muy agringado, ya no es Juan Palomares. ¡Ahora se llama Johnny Pigeonhouse!"[10]

Such sly, if obvious, jibes were inserted as fillers in many sketches. What usually brought down the house were jokes based on misunderstandings of language. As the Chicano folklorist José R. Reyna has noted, "Most jokes of this type are simply plays on words in Spanish, but a large number are of a cross cultural nature. That is, they involve erros of pronunciation and the ensuing misunderstanding due to ignorance of English or Spanish. The significance of these jokes is that they allow the Chicano to exalt his own position over the Anglo and the Mexican, neither of whom understands both languages."[11] *Carpa* humor functioned beyond mere diversion, becoming a chronicle of social processes.

The penniless urban roustabout living by his wits acquired a rounded configuration in the stage persona of the *pelado*.[12] First appearing in the *carpas* around Mexico City, the *pelado* employed a comic style based on pyrotechnical displays of verbal wit well suited to the Chicano sensibility. He soon became a staple in *carpa* productions within the United States. The *pelado*, portrayed as a feisty underdog, was prominently featured in sketches where his ironic commentary on social reality gained expressive power through a hybrid linguistic mixture of English, Spanish and *barrio caló*.

Such *pelados* as Don Catarino, Don Chema, Don Slico, Don Fido or El Bato Suave usually dressed with baggy pants, a battered hat and sometimes carried a slapstick. Acting broadly with much emphasis on corporeal movement, *pelados* starred in routines that were at once festive and indulgent, while also aggressive and hostile.

As a *portavoz* of group consciousness, the *pelado* assumed the role of a symbolic Chicano Everyman. His comic routines "became a sounding board for the culture conflict that Mexican-Americans felt in language usage, assimilation to American tastes and lifestyle, discrimination in the United States and *pocho* status in Mexico."[14] Consistently using code-switching, the *pelado* became a precursor in defining a bilingual, bicultural sensibility.

A popular *carpa* sketch title, "Cabrestea o Se Ahorca,"[15] presented in the 1930s, is a clear example of comedy used for social purpose. In it, a *mexicano* from the interior and a *pelado* from the States tackle the important issue of self-identity and linguistic allegiance. The *pelado* begins:

> Comadre, al entrar aquí al pueblo, vide unas chavas de aquella melaza, voy a ver si a alguna de ellas le saco un *date* pa' llevarla a dar un *ride* y luego la llevo al mono y, si no quiere ir al mono, al menos le merco su *ice cream* de a *dime* pa' comenzar a darle ganchola. A ver si me da chanza pa' que se me quite la pelota de la otra.

The dialogue continues with the *pelado's* masterful deployment of codeswitching. The final message, given by the *pelado's comadre* in Mexico, is a vision of the Chicano as linguistically insufficient and culturally incomplete.

> Bueno, que así hablen los de allá está bueno, pero usted es mexicano y ahora está usted en México y, si no quiere que le tomen el pelo, hable usted con la gente. Recuerde que el deber de todo ciudadano honrado y decente

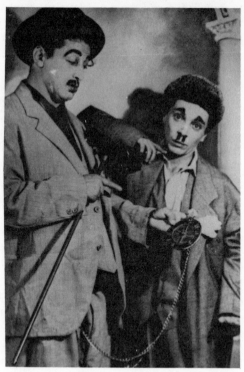

Don Catarino. **Don Suave and Don Lalo.**

es perfeccionar su vocabulario para que se le tome como persona educada. No hay que corromper con disparates nuestro precioso idioma, así es que una de dos: o se corrige o se devuelve, porque aquí estamos completos.

For Chicano audiences, the message was clear although many-sided. On the one hand, the sketch forced them to recognize that acculturation to Anglo norms and mores was an inevitable, if painful, reality. On the other hand, the forceful rendition of their vernacular and world view through the commanding figure of the *pelado* underscored an assertive, even if incipient stand countering Mexican linguistic and cultural hegemony.

Carpa sketches were creative responses to conflicting cultural loyalties and projected varied responses to problems of acculturation, cultural sustenance and ethnic solidarity. Cavorting through them all, the scrappy *pelado* who survives by his wits escaping calamity by "the seat of his pants," touched tap roots of recognition in audiences immersed in the daily battles of survival.

The "funky" milieu of the *carpa* engendered its pervasive aesthetic, *rascuachismo,* a way of confronting the world from the perspective of the downtrodden, the rebel, the outsider. To be *rascuachi* is to possess an ebullient spirit of irreverence and insurgency, a carnivalesque topsy-turvy vision where authority and decorum serve as targets for subversion. This defiant stance of the *carpa* is well summarized by Ignacio Lanzillot:

> "Pero allí por las calles, por los caminos, anda la carpa, viene y se va. Nace de la mimesis, del espíritu fársico, del escape colectivo y de la risa. Sus constantes: la improvisación, la imagen grotesca del grupo humano del que nace, sus mitos y anhelos, su paisaje limpio o sucio, la crítica política, la burla a los vicios sociales, el canto desafinado, el baile descuadrado, la acrobacia raquítica, el albur insolente."[16]

Essentially a form of entertainment for the masses, *carpas* helped to define and sustain ethnic and class consciousness. Their robust ribaldry and rebellious instincts were wedges of resistance against conformity and prevailing norms of middle-class decency within Chicano communities. *Carpas* motivated and helped establish a new sense of self-identity for the Mexican American in the Southwest by a) valorization and vitalization of Chicano vernacular, especially incipient forms of code-switching; b) elaboration of a critical mode exemplified in the anti-establishment stance of the *pelado;* c) maintenance of oral tradition and humor in its various modalities as a cultural weapon applied symbolically to annihilate and vanquish oppressors; d) elaboration of a down-to-earth, direct aesthetic deeply imbedded in social tradition.

As a small, often family-based unit, the resilient *carpa* survived the depression, repatriations and World War II. Having cultivated loyal audiences in remote rural areas and on the outskirts of urban *barrios, carpas* survived well into the 1940s. La Carpa Mantecón, Carpa Modelo, Carpa Cubana, Carpa Escalona and Carpa García among many others, were all examples of a genuine "poor theatre." On an empty portable stage with minimal props and a reliance on the most ancient skills of mimicry, clowning and lampooning, *carperos* anchored the imaginations of their audiences to social reality. It was a theatre of escape but also a reminder, an art of transcendence having an intimate relationship with human life that deeply penetrated the soil of popular culture.

Tandas de Variedad

The popular etymology of vaudeville might be in the phrase *voix de ville* or voice of the city streets. In its democratic character and kaleidoscopic, fluid form highlighting popular idioms of acting, dancing and singing, vaudeville gave impetus to an emerging urban sensibility. In Chicano communities, the stage equivalent to American vaudeville were the *tandas de variedad*.

While the *carpa* derived mainly from circus traditions, *variedades* sprang from the varied forms of the *teatro de género chico* including *zarzuela,* operetta, *sainetes,* the critically parodic style of the *fin diseurs* in the European *café concerts* and most directly from the Mexican tradition of the *teatro de revista*.

After the Revolution of 1910, in the heady period when artists, writers and intellectuals were occupied in defining the essence of *lo mexicano*, the *teatro de revista* played a crucial role in projecting from the stage, the popular base of an emerging national culture. Urban folk types, vernacular language and a defiant anti-establishment tone were essential components of the *revistas* which played to audiences representing all strata of Mexican society. As the great muralist José Clemente Orozco affirms:

"¿Qué el teatro en México no existe? Sí existe y ha existido el teatro de Beristáin, La Rivas Cacho, Soto, los escenógrafos Galván y mil más "soldados desconocidos," y lo más curioso es que este teatro comenzó en 1910 ¡también! Antes de que los pintores pintarrajearan y se holgaran con repeticiones de ejidos y matracas zapatistas, héroes y tropa formada, ya Beristáin y la famosa Amparo Pérez; la Rivas Cacho y tantos más, 'servían' a las masa auténticas obras proletarias de un sabor y una originalidad inigualadas, ya se habían creado "El Pato Cenizo," "El País de la Metralla," 'Entre las Ondas,' 'Los Efectos de la Onda' y millares más, en donde lo que menos importaba era el libreto y la música, pues lo esencial era la interpretación, la compenetración de los actores con el público, formado éste de boleros chafiretes, gatas, mecapaleros; auténticos proletarios en galería, rotos, catrines, militares, prostitutas, ministros e intelectuales en luneta."[17]

Being politically partisan, the *revista* functioned as a tribunal for the debate of national issues. Its essence was an acerbic, critical stance personified in the irreverent *pelado* and the insouciant *vedette* (singer-dancer-actress) both of whom added a sparkling levity to serious social concerns. It was this light touch expressed in witty plots, hummable music and memorable, if somewhat risqué jokes that made it possible for the *revista* to survive the various post-revolutionary regimes in Mexico and cross the border into the Southwest.

The period of the 1920s and 30s was a golden era for Spanish-language theatre in the Southwest.[18] By 1926, Los Angeles had eight theatres exclusively devoted to the presentation of diverse forms of Spanish-language drama. An old-time resident recalls,

"En aquellos ocho teatros mexicanos ubicados en el centro de la Ciudad, de la Placita a la Primera, por la Main, sin contar el gran Teatro Mason donde trabajaba la Fábregas, en los teatros de vecindad, se presentaban óperas, zarzuelas, drama, comedia, bailes, variedades, todo en español. Los espectadores reían sanamente con las geniales payasadas del morcillero y graciosísimo actor cómico, Romualdo Tirado, y con la inigualable gracia de la Pingüica, Lupe Rivas Cacho, un cachote de picardía mexicana enjabonada, enjuagada y planchadita. Los ocho teatros mexicanos de la Main y los de los aledaños se aprestaban de espectadores, diariamente, noche a noche y algunos trabajando en matinés sábados y domingos."[19]

Waiting patiently in long lines, the spectators were dazzled by the thousands of electric lights brilliantly lighting the *marquesinas* announcing international stars like the great doyenne of the Mexican theatre, Virginia Fábregas, the renowned Cuban *cupletista,* Pilar Arcos, the premier *declamadora,* Bertha Singerman, from Buenos Aires, and such new crowd pleasers as Dolores del Río, Ramón Navarro and Tito Guízar. From Paris, Barcelona, Madrid, Buenos Aires, La Habana and Mexico City, the cavalcade of stars always included Mexican American performers who began developing their own legions of fans.

The avid theatre-goers were a heterogeneous group, yet all expected the *teatros* to mirror their reality and their beliefs. During this period of the twenties and thirties, the *mexicanos de acá de este lado* possessed two distinct mind sets regarding their relationship to Anglo-American and Mexican culture forms.[20] Those newly arrived after the violence of the Revolution had a refugee mentality and saw themselves as temporary visitors in the United States. For them, the resident Mexican Americans were seen as dispossessed of their ancestral heritage and dismissed as *pochos.* A second group, the long-established *Tejanos, Manitos, Californios,* had long since accomodated themselves to struggle and survival within a bicultural environment. The younger generation from both groups was the one which most creatively responded to the new reality in the assumption of a bi-sensibility that transformed and re-contextualized cultural elements from both cultures in a new synthesis. This incipient form of bicultural awareness becomes especially evident in the *tandas de variedad* with their eclectic mixture of styles, forms and language freely borrowed from Anglo-American burlesque and vaudeville and from the diverse Mexican traditions of the *teatro de género chico*. This inventive *melange* is evident in a program from the Teatro Cine Zaragoza in San Antonio, Texas, for Sunday, May 8, 1932, that announces the company of La Chata Noloesca with the following program:[21]

Atracciones Noloesca

1. La Revista en un acto titulada; Instantáneas
2. Fox Los Modelos por Anita Islas y Lola Martínez
3. Fantasía Mexicana por el bailarín Ramón González
4. Mexicanerías por la Chata Noloesca
5. Sketch de Risa Loco
6. Deliriando-baile por Ramón González
7. Fox Rosita por La Chata y Lola Martínez, la Maja, Anita Islas
8. Rosa por todo el Cuadro
9. La Plata de Ameca: Conjunto Final

Harmoniously blending staged versions of the fox trot, a short *revista,* Mexican folk dances and sketches tinged with folkloric elements, the program presents an overt intent to reach the various cultural allegiances represented in the audience. This aim at bridging two cultures becomes a constant in Mexican American popular theatre.

Working-class origin was a reality that cut across generational and residence patterns. A vast majority of both the refugee and settled *mexicano* populations belonged to the working sector, be they urban or rural. Another common denominator was tenacious adherence to some rather static and romantic notions of what constituted *lo mejicano*. According to a long-time resident of Los Angeles, "la patria estaba en su Virgen de Guadalupe, en sus enchiladas, sus tamales y sus frijoles refritos en su jarabe, sus *Chiapanecas,* su *Abandonado* y su *Dios nunca muere*. Iban en busca de su Cónsul como en busca de su padre."[22] It was the Mexican Consulate, along with the mutual aid societies, that sponsored civic celebrations, fiestas and parades. The Consulates in Chicago, Detroit, Los Angeles and other cities with large concentrations of Mexican Americans promoted art exhibitions of the Mexican mural masters, hosted receptions for visiting writers and intellectuals and kept alive rather static and class-bound notions of *lo mexicano*.

Popular theatre functions importantly as a wedge of resistance to "official" cultural norms. *Revistas* criticized and lampooned those in power and their institutions, and through the stock character of the *pelado,* projected a minority view of prevailing social conditions. The very diversity and syncretic form of the *tandas de variedad* approximated the class divisions of the Spanish-speaking community with divergent values, loyalties and consciousness. *Tandas* captured a new spirit as Chicanos became urbanized, and as mass media (movies, radio and the recording industry) started to replace the most intimate forms of oral tradition and communal folk practices.

By the 1920s, *tandas de variedad* alternating with Mexican- or Hollywood-made movies (3 shows a day, 4 on week-ends) were the staple fare of the Spanish-speaking vaudeville circuit spanning the Southwest. A glimpse into this world at the Nacional and Zaragoza theatres in San Antonio, Texas, is vividly portrayed by an old time trouper:

> "Se presentaban tres tandas diarias y cuatro los fines de semana. No había día de descanso. A las segundas se les pagaba siete dólares por semana, ocho a las de línea y un poco más a las solistas.
> Aunque pagaban muy poco, la empresa proporcionaba el vestuario para el *show*. Solamente las solistas tenían que poner su propio vestuario. Nosotras las de la línea sí teníamos que tener pares de zapatos negros, blancos, plateados y dorados.
> En un número, *Lindo Michoacán*, salíamos en bataclán sin mallas con

enormes bateas decoradas de Michoacán que movíamos al compás de la música, moviendo el cuerpo lentamente en diversas figuras coreografiadas. [. . .] Otro número se llamaba *Los Dorados de Villas*. Me acuerdo muy bien que usabamos unos enormes sombreros galoneados que brillaban con escarcha."[23]

Production numbers alluding to folkloric themes became so popular that a special form, *cuadros de evocación* developed. Their intent was to create evocations of an edenic agrarian past at the moment of exodus to the cities. Urban cultural shock, employment discrimination and acculturation pressures could be momentarily put aside as the *tandas* presented idealized visions of rural life with archetypal figures like the campesino and his *trigueña* happily working on their *milpa*. A hit song of the time, *Canción Mixteca* by José López Alvarez, became an instant classic and struck the dominant tone:

"Qué lejos estoy del suelo donde he nacido
Inmensa nostalgia invade mi pensamiento
Y al verme tan solo y triste cual hoja al viento
Quisiera llorar, quisiera morir de sentimiento."

Nostalgia for the popular, related to the romantic sensibility of much folk literature consumed by Mexican Americans was not totally negative. The emotive, melodramatic mode of the *cuadros de evocación* underscored a heightened sympathetic relationship to all things Mexican. This fierce loyalty could lead to a positive and assertive ethnic identification countering the massive efforts towards cultural homogenization exerted by all institutions of the dominant culture.

Conforming to the madcap, giddy pace of the period, *tanda* repertoire was effervescent and optimistic. The songs were lively, the laughs were loud, dancing was frenzied and the dominant mood was cosmopolitan. Above all, there was a spirit of emancipation for women. In the United States, suffragettes clamored for judicial and political power while flappers stood up for sexual and personal autonomy. In Mexico, viable exponents of emerging feminine freedom were the *vedettes*, the audacious singer-dancer-actresses of the *teatro frívolo*. With their bold and saucy routines, they questioned sanctified codes of modesty and decorum.

Couplés from María Conesa, "La Gatita Blanca," such as her famous, "Ay morrongo, morrongo, morrongo, me lo quito, me lo pongo," had the same delicious effect on the *respetable público*, whether at the Teatro Colón in Mexico City or the Teatro Mason in Los Angeles, California. And when the wondrous *vedette*, Celia Montalbán, pranced along the runway intoning her light-hearted version of "Mi Querido Capitán" at the Liceo in Mexico City, the song was soon echoed in *tandas de variedad* from Detroit to San Antonio, Texas: "Soy capitán primero, el más valiente del batallón, pero cuando enamoro, soy general y de división . . . Ay, Ay, Ay, Ay, mi querido capitán . . ."[24]

The lightness and frivolity on stage was ephemeral. Outside the theatre, *La crisis*, the Great Depression raged, forcing Chicanos to go hungrier than usual as they organized protests and stood patiently in interminable relief lines. Soon thereafter, the repatriations of the 1930s dispersed families and created widespread distress as 300,000 *mexicanos* were deported across the border to Mexico, despite the fact that significant numbers were United States citizens. The acute social situation gave rise to more politically partisan *revistas*, like *Los Efectos de la Crisis* and *Los Repatriados*, written by Don Catarino Perrín.[25] The *cuadros de evocación* also became less nostalgic and more focused on real conditions.

The Second World War became a historical watershed for Mexican Americans. A hit song of the period immensely popular in the *tandas de variedad* projects the patriotic mood:

> "Me voy de solado razo
> Voy a ingresar a las filas
> Con los valientes muchachos que
> dejan novias queridas
> Que dejan madres llorando,
> llorando su despedida."

Rousing production numbers featured khaki-clad chorines prancing to choreographed military close-order drills. *Tandas* often ended with the playing of the Mexican and the American national anthems as the audience stood silently at attention. Half a million Chicano servicemen marched off to fight in the Pacific, France, Sicily and North Africa. Heriocally serving their country, those who survived returned home to witness the infamous zoot-suit riots that rocked Los Angeles from June 4 to 10, 1943.

The barrio and its denizens create a new mythology and new archetypes in the popular theatre. *Variedades* retain their old spirit of levity but a biting, ironic tinge enters the humor. The *pachuco* in the United States and his counterpart, the *tarzán* in Mexico, become new incarnations of the *pelado*. Whether in songs, monologues or sketches, the *pachuco* materializes as a manifold arbiter of urban sensibility. In his dress, stance and, above all, his speech, the *pachuco* symbolizes both cultural conflict and resistance.

Eclipsing the stage, movies and the recording industry become potent new mediators of group consciousness by the mid 1940s. The *canción ranchera*, an urban genre nostalgically hankering back to rural themes, becomes the new musical vogue. As the silver screen creates new idols, headliners from the *variedades* are relegated to secondary status by a public clamoring to see and applaud Jorge Negrete, Pedro Infante, Blanca Estela Pavón and a host of other stars of the Mexican

The Mason Theatre.

Tin Tan as pachuco.

cinema who made lucrative grand tours throughout the Southwest.

The younger generation of urbanized Chicanos grew less satisfied with the simple homespun dimension of the *variedades* after savoring the expanded entertainment potential of the movies. Furthermore, it was economically more expedient for theatre owners to rent and screen a movie several times a day than to sustain a company of live performers. Audiences diminished, movie screenings increased, and soon the stage footlights were extinguished. Recalling the demise, an old trouper muses:

> "Fíjese que todo esto fue muriendo poco a poco, cuando empezaron las películas, comenzaron a quitar las variedades. Entonces, llegó un momento en que ya no ponían variedades, nada más película y película . . . y se acabó todo el show . . . Quitaron hasta los pianos de los teatros. Antes, llegaba cualquier compañía, aunque fuera nomás con pianista, y listos para el espectáculo. Después ya quitaron hasta los pianos . . .[26]

Tenaciously hanging on, small Mexican American troupes struggled on well into the 1950s, following the migrant stream and performing in church halls, community centers and old theatres. Television dealt the final blow: "¿Sabe qué vino a matar todo esto, la televisión? Mató todo lo que fue *show business*. Ya tenían el espectáculo en la casa, ya no iban a los teatros. ¿A qué? después todo terminó."[27]

[1] For a historical analysis of the various sub-genres of the *farándula* or *teatro frívolo*, see Armando María y Campos, *El Teatro de Género Chico en la Revolución Mexicana* (México: Biblioteca del Instituto Nacional de Estudios Históricos de la Revolución Mexicana, 1956).

[2] From an interview with Sr. J. Rivera from Austin, Texas. The recording was done June 15, 1973 in Washington, D.C.

[3] From an interview with Sr. Raúl Salinas, June 10, 1974, Austin, Texas.

[4] From an interview with Sr. Alex Aguilar, August 12, 1983, Guadalupe Community Center, San Antonio, Texas.

[5] Alfredo de la Torre, "La Carpa García," *Caracol*, Julio 1978, pp. 5-7; for anecdotal material on La Carpa García see Ben King, "Awakening Guadalupe's Ghost." *San Antonio News*, Sunday, July 26, 1981. pp. 8-14.

[6] From the interview with Sr. Alex Aguilar on August 12, 1983.

[7] Peter Brook, *The Empty Space* (New York: Atheneum 1968). pp. 66-67.

[8] Roberto Blanco Moheno, "El Mundo de la Carpa," *Siempre*, Número 1489, 6 de enero de 1982, p. 29.

[9] This form of humor is discussed in Mihail Bakhtin's *Rabelais and His World*, Tr. Helene Iswolsky (Cambridge: M.I.T. Press, 1968).

[10] From the interview with Sr. Alex Aguilar.

[11] José R. Reyna, *Raza Humor, Chicano Joke Traditions in Texas* (San Antonio: Penca Books, 1980). See especially the texts in the section, "Jokes Based on Misunderstandings of Language," pp. 41-45.

[12] See Samuel Ramos, *Profile of Man and Culture in Mexico* (Austin: University of Texas Press 1962).

[13] Armando María y Campos, p. 365.

[14] Nicolás Kanellos, "The Mexican American Circus," *Collected Writings from the Hertzberg Circus Project*, ed. by Susan J. Frieband (San Antonio: Institute for Intercultural Studies and Research, 1982), p. 30.

[15] La Compañía de Variedades Netty y Jesús Rodriguez performed this sketch in the Southwest circa 1930. A version is recorded in Arhoolie Folklyric Records #9021.

[16] Ignacio Lanzillot, "La Carpa" n.d.n.p.

[17] This letter by José Clemente Orozco is cited in Margo Sus, "El teatro de revista," *Revista mexicana de ciencias políticas y sociales*, Año XXV, Nueva Epoca, Enero-Junio, 1979 numero 95-96. See also, Aurelio de los Reyes, "Del Blanquita del público y del género chico mexicano," *Diálogo*, El Colegio de Mexico, Num. 92 Marzo-Abril 1980, p. 31. Relevant information on the current status of *Teatro de revista* in Mexico is found in, *Textos 9-10*, Revista Bimestral Del Departamento de Bellas Artes Del Gobierno De Jalisco, Guadalajara, México, Año 2, Nos. 9-10, 1975.

[18] See Nicolás Kanellos, "The Flourishing of Hispanic Theatre in the Southwest," *Latin American Theatre Review* 16/1 (Fall, 1983), 29-40.

[19] Rafael Trujillo Herrera, "Del Teatro y de la Vida, Los Angeles, extensión de Mexico." *La Opinión*, Los Angeles, Domingo 15 de Marzo de 1981, p. 12.

[20] For a thorough discussion of this problematic, see Américo Paredes, "The Pocho Appears," *A Texas Mexican Cancionero* (Urbana: University of Illinois Press, 1976) pp. 153-161.

[21] From a program in the personal archives of Belia Areu Camargo, San Antonio. Texas.

[22] Rafael Trujillo Herrera, op. cit.

[23] From an interview with Sra. Susi Astol, June 12, 1980. San Antonio, Texas.

[24] For an evocative account of the *gran vedettes* in Mexico see Carlos Monsiváis, *Celia Montalván (Te brindas, voluptuosa e imprudente)* (Mexico: Secretaría de Educación Pública, Martín Casillas Editores, S.A., 1983). See also the marvelous photographic catalog, *La Fárandula en México 1908-1925*, (México: Centro de Información Gráfica del Archivo General de la Nación, 1982).

[25] Nicolás Kanellos provides significant information on Mexican American dramaturges in "Flourishing . . .," op. cit.

[26] From an interview with Sra. Belia Areu Camargo, December 4, 1981. San Antonio, Texas.

[27] Belia Areu Camargo, op. cit.

TEATRO HISPANO

CALLE 116 y QUINTA AVENIDA   UNiversity 4 - 8066

VIERNES 30 a JUEVES 5 de SEPT. - 1946

Sept. 6 al 12 En la Pantalla "EL NIÑO DE LAS MONJAS"

Septiembre 13 al 19 En la Pantalla "MARIQUILLA TERREMOTO"

EN ESCENA
QUINTA SEMANA DE EXITO DE

LA CHATA NOLOESCA

Con su Nuevo Cuadro de Variedades en el que Figura la Simpática y Encantadora Vedette

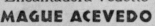

MAGUE ACEVEDO

El Apuesto Charro Mexicano

DON - ROLANDO

Los Actores y Comediantes Mexicanos

EL GRAN RAMIRIN y Don **CHEMA**

Las Simpáticas y Lindas Bailarinas
María Luisa Alvarez - Nena Vázquez
Gilda Markin y Livia Cadena
En la Sensacional Revista Musical

"MEXICO de mis AMORES"

EN LA PANTALLA

Agustín IRUSTA y Amelia BENCE
en EL MATRERO

LOYAL PRESS, 778 Prospect Avenue, Bronx 55, N. Y.

Jorge A. Huerta

Labor Theatre, Street Theatre and Community Theatre in the Barrios, 1965-1983

Chicano theatre groups since 1965 often encompass all three of the above definitions: many are community-based theatres dealing with labor issues performed in the streets of the barrio. Beyond these distinctions, we can also distinguish the student groups from those above, although they can also produce plays or actos that are labor-oriented and are performed in the streets. Then there are the community-based groups that include students, children and working adults—so where do they find their definition? Essentially, Chicano theatre in this epoch can be divided into a variety of categories, from student to professional, and within that broad range we can find some groups that fit nicely into the standard definitions listed in the title of this essay. There are other theatre groups that defy strict lines of categorization and have to be studied as individual phenomena. In each case, these teatros have made and continue to make an impact on their communities and remain important examples of the kind of Chicano theatre that flourished after 1965.

When Luis Valdez founded the Teatro Campesino in 1965 under the wing of César Chávez's then incipient farm labor union, the talented young playwright, actor and director began a theatre group that immediately recalled the labor theatres of the 1930s in this country. Here was a group of striking farmworkers re-creating their daily struggles for each other and for other audiences as well. This was true workers' theatre: a theatre composed of workers, not actors, performing for other laborers just like them. The common theme of "Join the Union!" and *Huelga!* ("Strike!") reminded theatre historians of Clifford Odets' much acclaimed *Waiting for Lefty*. Like Odets' dramatization the early actos of the Teatro Campesino called for a strike as their conclusion/solution. But while the audiences witnessing "Lefty" might have been inclined to follow the actors outside the theatre with clenched fists and the cry of "Strike! Strike! Strike!" emanating from their mouths, they were, after all, just theatre goers caught-up in the emotions of the moment. They were not practicing farmworkers, having just spent the day on the picket lines in hopes of improving their lifestyle. Valdez' troupe was seen with awe by audiences all across the country and as far abroad as Nancy, France, as humble workers fought in a struggle against the most powerful lobby in California: the wealthy growers.

The early actos were seen as modern morality plays, complete with allegorical figures and clearly defined distinctions between the heroes (striking farmworkers) and the villains (growers, scabs and labor contractors). Having gotten his basic training with the still youthful San Francisco Mime Troupe the previous summer, Valdez went to the union headquarters with a clear sense of what a labor theatre should be: didactic, yet funny, bombastic and bold, bawdy and poignant all at once. Having been born to a migrant farmworker family in the very town Chávez based his efforts, Valdez was not new to the cause; he had lived it as a child and had been one of the few to escape the inevitable fate of defeat, poverty and unrealized dreams. His dream of a theatre that educated as it entertained, that spread the news about the Union's efforts, was soon realized.

This early worker's theatre remains the only true example of a labor theatre of sustaining value in our era. Because Valdez was not only attuned to the needs of his audiences as striking farmworkers and also aware of the problems he and his raggle-taggle troupe collectively created, he succeeded in creating a vivid example of what a group of committed workers can do with nothing more than "two boards and a passion." This was drama that could be performed in theatres or in the very fields which sowed the misery the actors dramatized, satirized and sang about. Marching behind the banner of the *Virgen de Guadalupe* from Delano to Sacramento in 1966, the unionizers and their sympathizers were treated each evening to the songs and actos of Valdez's troupe in a style reminiscent of revival meetings or of the earliest dramatizations to reach what is now the Southwest in the sixteenth century. That early missionary theatre found a new expression during that long march: the banner of the gentle Virgin followed by the symbol of the farmworkers' union. This was ritual theatre, political theatre and mythical theatre performed along Highway 99, like a modern recreation of the Crusades. From one community to another, sometimes performing in parking lots and sometimes indoors, the Teatro Campesino established itself as the outward symbol of a workers' struggle.

But this early example of a workers' theatre could not last, for Valdez had to choose the Teatro over the Union. He discovered that the unionizing efforts were keeping him and his troupe from developing fully as a theatre group. In choosing to move away from Chávez, both literally and symbolically, Valdez was re-defining his theatre, changing its course while never altering its name. Even before that difficult decision, the Teatro Campesino had begun to adopt the goals and techniques of street theatre as well as spiritual drama. When the troupe performed outdoors, in parks or parking lots, in fields and factories, the Teatro Campesino knew what it was to be a street theatre. Like other street theatres of the epoch, many dedicated to ceasing United States involvement in Vietnam, the Teatro Campesino found itself performing in the face of the "enemy," poised on its flatbed truck within earshot (gunshot) of local gendarmes eager to cause a little destruction. Members of the troupe at that time recall how they had to be constantly wary of the threat of violence, and how the term "stagefright" took on a new meaning in the face of goon squads and fully garbed riot police.

The very term "street theatre" connotes a political act, and that is just what the Teatro Campesino symbolized, whether the message was overtly political or symbolically spiritual. This was theatre in the streets, touring from barrio-to-barrio throughout the country with missionary fervor, but this time the message was "social justice" rather than spiritual salvation. Like its counterparts throughout the nation and indeed the world, the Teatro Campesino was dedicated to improving man's lot at home and abroad. With thoughts of farmworkers' problems always fresh in their minds, the Teatro's members created actos that condemned the government for its involvement in Vietnam, and even cautiously criticized other Chicanos for joining the armed forces and going to the war.

Not long after the Teatro Campesino began touring, other groups formed as if in response to individual communities' separate issues. Originally, these troupes emerged from the growing ranks of Chicano university and college students in the late sixties and early seventies. Many of these developing groups modeled their actos after the Campesino's examples, and a few went on to become community-based teatros, eager to follow in the footsteps of Valdez's troupe, but with sometimes varying issues to dramatize. Once again, the distinctions become blurred if one considered Guadalupe Saavedra's Teatro Chicano, based in Los Angeles in the late 1960s. This teatro was a community-based, mostly student group under Saavedra's direction, he a mature man beyond school age.

But if the group was young, one of its actos, *Justice*, was not for the young at heart. This simple acto written by Saavedra, dramatizes the control of the people by a "town father" called Honkey Sam, who uses his "dogs" to keep his workers docile and helpless. When a young girl is killed by one of the "dogs," the people finally tire of this abuse and overcome their oppressor. The Teatro Campesino's early calls for "Strike!"

are here replaced by "Fight back!" and the short, simple acto ends with the birth of a new savior: Che Guevara. Because the characters are Honkey Sam's workers, Saavedra's group could be seen as a workers' theatre, but with street theatre techniques. Curiously, the author describes the final tableaux of the birth like a Madonna and Christ-child posing, thus also calling to mind the liturgical dramas that preceded all other styles in the barrio.

The majority of Chicano theatre groups of the period from 1965 to the mid-seventies were capable of performing outdoors, on the streets proper or in other alfresco situations. The themes varied from drug abuse, to problems in the schools, to police brutality, but they were almost always oriented to the communities from which the groups emanated. Certainly the problems were the same from one barrio to the next, and touring teatros were always sorry to discover that things were no better in the next town. If the city police were brutalizing youths in the urban settings, it was the country sheriffs who were beating up the kids outside of the city limits. Regardless of different titles and other-colored uniforms, the conditions never changed. The teatros remained militant in their response to the situations in their communities and maintained a street theatre pose throughout their sometimes brief existence or until their efforts were turned to developing aesthetics rather than politics.

Three groups in Los Angeles best exemplify the evolution from street theatre to community theatre: Teatro Movimiento Primavera, Teatro Obrero and Teatro Urbano. Teatro Urbano was the first of these groups to develop, under the direction of René Rodríguez. From the beginning, this teatro was dedicated to a community effort, attracting its members from the surrounding barrios of East Los Angeles in the early seventies. The group's name defines the issues it chose to dramatize, working in the same style as so many other groups that followed in the Teatro Campesino's famous footsteps. Once again, most of the members were young, although not all were in school, thus distinguishing the Teatro Urbano from student groups of the period. Instead, this could be called a community theatre group, interested in creating plays and actos that expressed the realities of the urban environment.

After the Urbano's early efforts, the Teatro Obrero and Teatro Movimiento Primavera were also formed, with sometimes dual member-ships from group-to-group and co-produced events that found individu-als participating in more than one group's work. Under the direction of Guillermo Loo, Movimiento Primavera evolved from Marxist ideology to Aristotelian theory over the course of several years. Himself a student at the University of California at Los Angeles, Mr. Loo's evolution from "Politics before Art" to "Art before Politics" echoed the transforma-tions of other groups. Many teatros began to see their role as community

Los Angeles' El Teatro Urbano.   **Teatro Movimiento Primavera.**

leaders in a different light during the late seventies. The war in Vietnam had ended long ago, the civil rights movement had dissipated beyond recognition, and the never-fully-defined Chicano Movement had also been lost to divisive forces along the way. With this reality staring them coldly in the face, these groups had to reassess their role as community theatres. The community, they discoverd, had stopped coming to teatro presentations, somehow no longer interested in the issues of earlier years.

It was as if the Chicano and Mexican communities were mirroring the broader society in the evolving "me" generation, with economic hardship all about and the daily burdens of working and raising families. Conditions had not changed for the better in the barrios; all the problems that early teatros had dramatized were still as pressing. But the teatros had to realize that only the initiated were going to performances, and although these patrons were to be treasured and rewarded, there were many more people out there who needed to be reached. Today, members of the three original groups participate in mutual activities, although Teatro Obrero is no longer in existence. Some members of that group have joined other teatros such as the now professional Teatro de la Esperanza, of Santa Barbara, while others work with Rodríguez or Loo when called upon. Mr. Loo is teaching Chicano theatre at California State University at Los Angeles and Rodríguez and his wife Rosemary continue to produce theatre in their own center, involving members of the surrounding community.

In the dominant society, the term "community theatre" connotes a group of aficionados, amateurs, if you will, who love theatre and get together to produce plays. These companies are not lauded as adventurous, nor are they noted for high production standards. Seasons are selected from the safest Broadway comedies and not-too-serious melodramas with a special place for Neil Simon or Kaufmann and Hart in their repertoires. Not so when we talk about community theatre in the barrios, although there are some examples of this kind of fare in some larger Spanish-speaking populations. To practiced teatro followers, a community teatro reflects its community, creating scripts that reveal that community's ideosyncracies. For some, this can mean very political commentary, while for others a sense of community can be achieved through religious dramas.

The earliest theatre in this country was Spanish-language religious drama, and the state most noted for the preservation of this spiritual heritage is New Mexico. With such a long tradition of Spanish religious folk drama, it was only natural for residents of this state to adapt the spiritual themes to the political when the communities began to recognize the need for social change. In 1977, José Rodríguez, a professional actor from Puerto Rico, via New York, was invited to teach a theatre workshop at the Roman Catholic University of Albuquerque. Under the careful and patient guidance of this highly professional theatre artist, the Compañía de Teatro de Alburquerque* was eventually born. This group is an excellent example of a Chicano community theatre group, for it includes people from all walks of life, from age five to eighty in some productions. Because of Rodríguez's high standards, the group's work is very fine, but its members are not all trained in theatrical art.

When Rodríguez first arrived in Albuquerque, he chose plays by Lorca, scripts that he knew would succeed in their original language, because so many New Mexicans have maintained both Spanish and English in their daily lives. There is also a long tradition of Spanish culture in that state, with many descendants of the original settlers still living there. From those modern Spanish classics, Rodríguez then moved to original scripts by local authors and began to produce adaptations of traditional religious folk plays like *El Sueño del Santero (The Woodcarver's Dream)*, based on the famous and ubiquitous *Los Pastores (The Shepherds)*. Another original script by Denise Chávez was *Sí, Hay Posada (Yes, There Is Lodging)*, which deals with a modern family's conflicts during a traditional Christmas party. With seventeen actors whose ages ranged from five to eighty, this was community theatre of the highest order. Although few on the stage were trained actors, there was always a sense of the theatrical and never an element of insecurity. The audiences loved the production as well, for while recalling ancient folk custom, it addressed contemporary dilemmas, such as a Chicano Vietnam veteran's difficult readjustment to life back home.

El Teatro Desengaño del Pueblo (literally translated to mean "Telling it like it is") was founded in Gary, Indiana, in 1972 by Nicolás Kanellos

*In deference to the original spelling of the city's name, the teatro chose to include the missing "r."

67

El Teatro Desengaño.

El Teatro Campesino.

whose work with the Teatro Chicano of Austin, Texas, had prepared him to continue producing community theatre of relevance. Like the Albuquerque group, Kanellos' teatro was composed of children, workers and students, and was dedicated to exposing injustices in the region. Unlike Rodríguez's troupe, however, the Gary Teatro did not reach back to the early Spanish religious theatre, but plunged headlong into political isses such as government corruption. In contrast to Albuquerque's majestic mountain surroundings, Gary is an urban steel mill town, with constant clouds of black smoke to remind everyone of the major industry . . . and urban blight.

The Gary Teatro was unique for its time, intermingling children and adults, and also bringing together a variety of cultures including Chicanos, Mexicans, Puerto Ricans and Anglos. Its techniques were informed by the Teatro Campesino's early actos, and the collectively created works always pointed an accusing finger at real life counterparts of the villains onstage. Like the Albuquerque group, its goal was still messianic, couched in daily struggles between man and man rather than man and his cosmos. When Kanellos and various group members moved to Houston at the close of the seventies, the Teatro Desengaño del Pueblo became another fond memory for its audiences and perhaps a bitter remembrance for its nemeses.

Because this essay has focused on the three types of theatre delineated in the title, there has been no mention of the now professional Hispanic theatre groups in the Southwest. Groups such as the current Teatro Campesino, Teatro de la Esperanza, Bilingual Foundation of the

Arts in Los Angeles and Teatro Meta in San Diego have not been discussed, only because they have each gone beyond the limitations of the types of groups in question here. These teatros may or may not be based in their respective communities, but they have certainly addressed workers' themes; however, they are now considered professional rather than "community" theatres. From a variety of aesthetic and political spectrums, the professional teatros can be seen as logical extensions of the labor, street and community theatre movement.

Without that first step on the streets, in the community or at the side of the workers, none of these professional companies would have achieved professional standards. Lacking the community's support, the workers' interest and the issues of the street, today's teatros would be like any other theatre companies that do not address a particular group of people and their culture. Hundreds of years after the first Spanish drama was staged and eighteen years after the Teatro Campesino began the Chicano theatre movement, there is still theatre in the barrios, on the streets and in professional houses. Each of these groups has its purpose and we can only hope that they continue in their commitment.

Bibliography

"El Alcalde," *Revista Chicano-Riqueña*, 3 (Otoño 1973), 2-9.

"Las Avispas." *Revista Chicano-Riqueña*, 7 (Verano 1974), 8-10.

Bagby, Beth. "El Teatro Campesino; Interviews with Luis Valdez." *Tulane Drama Review*, 11 (summer 1967), 70-80.

"Las dos caras del patroncito." In *Actos*, ed. Luis Valdez. San Juan Bautista, *Cucaracha Press*, 1971, pp. 7-19.

Drake, Sylvie. "El Teatro Campesino: Keeping the Revolution on Stage." *Performing Arts Magazine*, September 1970, pp. 56-62.

Dukore, Bernard F. "The Brown Revolution." In his *Documents For Drama and Revolution*. New York: Holt, Rinehard and Winston, 1971, pp. 211-13.

"Interview with Guadalupe de Saavedra." In his *Documents For Drama and Revolution*, pp. 214-20.

Gleason, Ralph J. "On the Town: Vital, Earthy and Alive Theater." *San Francisco Chronicle*, 4 May 1966, p. 41.

Huerta, Jorge A. "Chicano Agit-Prop; The Early Actos of El Teatro Campesino." *Latin American Theatre Review*, 11 (spring 1977), 45-58.

——————, *Chicano Theater: Themes & Forms*, Ypsilanti: Bilingual Press, 1982.

Jones, David R. "Farm Labor: Viva el Picket Sign." *New York Times*, 30 July 1967, sec. 4, p. 5.

Kanellos, Nicolás. "Chicano Theatre in the Seventies." *Theatre* (Yale) 12 (Fall 1980), 33-37.

"Fifty Years of Theatre in the Latino Communities of Northwest Indiana," *Aztlán*. 7 (Summer 1976), 255-65.

Loo, Guillermo. "Organizing Teatro." *Pláticas del Sexto Festival Nacional de los Teatros Chicanos*, 14-19 July 1975, pp. 10-11.

Lowell, Sondra. "El Teatro Campesino, Chicano Street Theatre." *Los Angeles Free Press*, 24 September 1971, p. 21.

McCoskey, Susan. "La Compañía de Teatro de Alburquerque," *The Drama Review*, 27 (Summer 1983), 50-60.

Moore, Jim. "Minority Theatre Branching Out: Increased Professionalism." *Los Angeles Times*, 11 May 1976, sec. 6, pp. 3, 5.

"New Grapes; El Teatro Campesino Performs for Migrant Farmworkers." *Newsweek*, 31 July 1967, p. 79.

"La quinta temporada." In *Guerilla Street Theater*, ed. Henry Lesnick. New York: Avon Books, 1973, pp. 197-212. Also in *Actos*, pp. 20-34; *Guerilla Theater*, ed. John Weisman. Garden City: Anchor Press/Doubleday, 1973, pp. 21-32.

Ramírez, Elizabeth Cantú. "The Annals of Chicano Theater: 1965-1973." M. A. thesis, University of California, Los Angeles, 1974.

"A Review of 'Silver Dollar': El Teatro Urbano en Florencia, N.M." *Floreciendo*, 1 (abril-mayo 1980), 11.

Saavedra, Guadalupe de. "Justice." In *Drama and Revolution*, ed. Bernard F. Dukore. New York: Holt, Rinehart and Winston, 1971, pp. 589-98.

"El teatro chicano de Austin." *Magazín*, October 1971, p. 43.

Margarita B. Melville
University of Houston

Female and Male in Chicano Theatre

In a survey of the outstanding Chicano theatre of the 1970s, found in three collections (Garza, 1976, Revista Chicano-Riqueña, 1979 and Morton, 1983), I searched for images of family relationships. Given the stated predominance of the family as a central value in Chicano culture, I was particularly interested in discovering how families are portrayed in the theatre. I found ample references and scenes depicting female-male relationships, but relatively few featuring parents and children or the relationships between individuals and their other consanguinal and affinal relatives. Grandparents were absent, except through indirect reference. Unfortunately, for my purpose, two outstanding plays produced by Teatro de la Esperanza, *Los Hijos* and *La Víctima* are not included in the two excellent collections I selected. First, I will comment on family relationships and then on female-male relationships.

Family Relationships

The role of mother is depicted in *Bernabé* by Luis Valdez. Bernabé is over thirty, but retarded and still under his mother's control. She actually uses him to work for their sustenance and to do errands. She controls him with the old adage, "The earth swallows up the children who don't respect their parents." She also claims that since Bernabé is her son, she still has the right to punish him, even though he is now a man.

A family group, consisting of a father, mother and daughter appear in *Rancho Hollywood*, by Carlos Morton. Don Rico, the governor, and his wife, Victoria, insist that their daughter Ramona should be respectful of them but bemoan the fact that she is not. The mother tries to intercede for her daughter when her father gets angry at her impertinence. Ramona, however, insists on speaking her mind and making her own decisions, thus demonstrating the generational gap between parents and children. Her parents just do not see things her way. She accuses

71

them, saying, "You are unbending as a mountain; no wonder all the youth are rebelling."

Luis Valdez, in *Bernabé*, features other kinship roles. He includes those of uncle, cousin and girl friend's brother. An uncle and a cousin are as close as a father and a brother. Bernabé's mother addresses her nephew, as "hijo" (son). He offers her some money and speaks to her with kindness and respect. He even gets angry when Torres laughs at her. Her nephew is not quite so tolerant with his uncle, but still treats him with special consideration. And cousins are like brothers. Primo says, "He is my cousin—sure he is crazy, but so what?" And he goes out of his way to be helpful to him.

The role of girl friend's brother is involved with the mythology that is Luis Valdez' forte and so is more difficult to analyze merely as a portrayal of a kinship role. Nevertheless, it does feature the role of a brother as protector of his sister's honor, as well as serving as an intermediary between her and his father. The father (the sun) approves of the marriage between his daughter (the earth) and Bernabé, once he has determined that Bernabé is an honorable man and loves her sincerely. The father, claiming that his daughter is a virgin, gives her in marriage to Bernabé. He blesses their union and tells them to have children, many children. Although the entire play is an allegory, the kinship roles are portrayed as life-like and represent the ideal in the stereotype of family relationships of traditional Mexican society.

The role of aunt is much like that of uncle. It parallels the role of mother. It is portrayed in *Brujerías* by Rodrigo Duarte-Clark. When Petra and Rafael go to see Tía Olga, she answers their knock by saying, "Entren, niños." Since Petra and Rafael, husband and wife, are adults, the phrase *niños* can be interpreted as *children*, meaning son and daughter. They come to visit her seeking personal and embarrassing advice since they have to admit that they are afraid of a witch. They come to her as one having the wisdom of old age, much like a mother.

The relationship of uncle and niece, as portrayed in Portillo's *The Day of the Swallows*, I will treat as a female-male relationship, rather than as a familial relationship. This is because the niece, Josefa, reveals a total absence of respect for her "shiftless" uncle. She does not treat him as a family member, but rather as an adversary male. I will therefore come back to their relationship in the next section.

Female and Male Relationships

In these plays I would classify female-male relationships in three possible categories: 1) partnership, 2) adversary with the male dominant, and 3) adversary with the female dominant. In a relationship of partnership, the female and male cooperate and share equally in the

Esperanza's *Brujerías*.

Rancho Hollywood,
by Carlos Morton.

decision-making process. In an adversary relationship there can be either a belligerent attitude or peaceful coexistence, but one or the other will dominate and make the decisions, while the other fights back unsuccessfully, seethes or accepts without rebuttal. In any case, it will be one or the other who is dominant and has the last word.

One of the most discouraging roles for a woman is that of the Secretary, Miss Jimenez, in *Los Vendidos* by Luis Valdez. This play is one of the earliest and most successful portrayals of the Chicano Movement. It features a Farmworker, a Pachuco youth, a Revolutionary and an assimilated "Mexican-American." It uses very effective stereotyping to illustrate the image of the Mexcian American generally held by the majority population. Its ending is a wonderful surprise. Except that in the end, the ultimate sell-out is the one female, the Secretary, the Chicana!

In Luis Valdez' other allegorical play, *Bernabé,* the role of mother is blended with that of the prostitute, Consuelo. Bernabé's one attempt to relate to a real woman becomes fraught with guilt. In the end there is no positive image of a woman, because La Tierra marries him, embraces him and buries him. She is a wonderful and idealistic figure, the land. There is a historical and vital idea in the conceptualization of what it means to be Mexican American. But La Tierra is not a woman. In the end, women are absent from this beautiful play except as a guilt-inflicting, exploitative and oppressive mother, a prostitute and an allegory of land, which means power.

I see the traditional role of women as portrayed in the majority of these plays as that of the wife who is not in the limelight herself, makes very few, if any, important decisions and contents herself with helping her husband and taking care of the children without making many demands on them for herself. Two plays present women in this role: *The Ultimate Pendejada* by Ysidro R. Macías and *El Rancho Hollywood* by Carlos Morton (especially the first version).

In *The Ultimate Pendejada*, the central figures are Robert and Mary, a young Chicano couple, who, during the course of the play come to accept their identity as Chicanos. In the first act they are a couple acculturated in Anglo society with a partnership-like relationship. The female has a slightly dominant role in that it is she who determines the schedule for intimate activity, having refused his tentative advances, while he meekly contents himself with helping with the dishes.

In the second act, a Chicano challenges Robert's manhood, his *machismo*, so he comes home and tells Mary that they are going to a meeting. All her entreaties and excuses are for naught. He has taken command of the situation. He becomes dominant, and she goes along. It is interesting to note that in order to illustrate the process of how a "Chicano identity" is acquired, the female-male relationship assumes a male-dominant adversary relationship. The change is gradual but by the third act, they have become María and Roberto. Roberto is firmly in charge and María thinks "he is so smart."

During a party in which three Chicano couples participate, there is an interesting sequence:

> Margarita: I'd like to get into Chicana Liberation. How about it, María . . . do you want to join?
> María: Chicana Liberation? What are they doing?
> Flor: Liberating Chicanas, of course. We've got to demand our rights from these *hombres!* They don't let us participate in anything!
> Emilio: Women's Liberation no vale caca! ¡Es una pendejada! How can you liberate yourselves from us when we are not liberated ourselves?
> Margarita: ¡Qué macho! If you guys don't let us participate, we're going to be against you, wait and see!
> Pancho: What would you rucas do to us?
> Flor: ¡A ver, a ver! How are you going to stay warm at night?

The above is an interesting perception and a historically accurate representation of the types of discussions regarding female liberation that went on during an early stage of the Chicano Movement. To be liberated meant to be allowed to participate; liberation had to come about for Chicanos first; and women hold power only in bed!

As their consciousness raising continues, María has all the questions and Roberto attempts to give the answers. The last scene is very telling. Roberto and María go to the *barrio* and talk to Chuey. He tells them that the answers to their questions are within themselves, they have to accept who and what they are and be true to themselves. But this last conversation, which explains that the ultimate stupidity is to change on the outside and remain the same inside, where it really counts, is only between Robert and Chuey. María stands there, by Robert's side, silent during the entire last crucial scene.

Morton has published two versions of *Rancho Hollywood*. It is difficult to analyze his portrayal of the female characters because of the historical allegory that is woven through. Still, female and male values and relationships are perceptible. The major difference between the two versions of the play is precisely the portrayal of the three females. The earlier version features a traditional treatment of female and male. Don Rico is the typical "macho." He is presented as a womanizer who takes advantage of Tonta, the Indian maid, and has two sons by her. He even threatens her, "I ought to slap your face!" To which she answers, "Don't you dare! I'll tell!" Of the three females, although exploited, she is certainly the one most in control of her situation! Although his wife thinks he has settled down considerably, she knew him to have been in his pursuit of women, "a demon, running amok with his eyes ablaze." She thinks he was wilder than his nephew Lorenzo. "He probably sees himself in Lorenzo and it aggravates him that he can't womanize anymore." Still, as Don Rico tells Tonta, "She's my lawful wedded wife and I love her dearly . . . pero, she has not the warmth, the passion that burns . . ."

In the second version of the play, Don Rico as "macho" is considerably toned down. His relationship to Tonta is omitted, and Don Rico and his wife, Victoria, are portrayed as a devoted couple, wherein the wife supports, counsels and accompanies him wherever he goes. She makes no mention of his previous sexual exploits. But true to her portrayal as a woman of a previous generation, she is, nevertheless, basically her husband's helpmate rather than a person in her own right.

Ramona, the daughter, on the other hand, is a product of a new generation searching for an identity outside that of her parents'. In the second version of the play, Ramona's part is considerably enhanced. It presents a take-charge woman on a par with Jed, who is the stereotype of the Anglo.

Two historical plays, *No Nos Venceremos* by Roberto J. Garza and *Los Dorados* by Carlos Morton deal with two traditional themes. *No Nos Venceremos* features the Mexican Revolution and presents a series of stereotyped characters that attempt to deal with the issue of class and liberation. The female figure is, of course, a *Soldadera*. True to the stereotype, she is a foul and loud mouthed female. She is overly concerned with *machismo*. She says they followed a leader because he was very *Macho* and, full of admiration, exclaims that another individual was very charming and *macho*. She is looking for a man, not yet appeared, who will be her *dueño*, which can be translated as boss or "owner." Because she is the only female figure, the reader or viewer is left with a

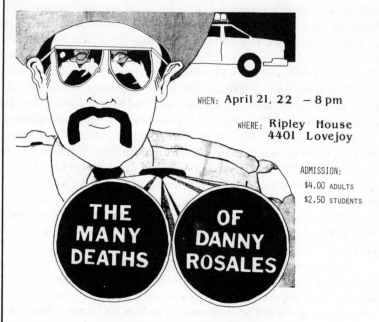

Get The Inside Story!

WHAT'S THE REAL TALE BEHIND THE NEW PLAY BY CARLOS MORTON ABOUT AN ACTUAL CASE OF POLICE BRUTALITY IN TEXAS?

WHEN: April 21, 22 — 8 pm

WHERE: Ripley House
4401 Lovejoy

ADMISSION:
$4.00 ADULTS
$2.50 STUDENTS

THE MANY DEATHS OF DANNY ROSALES

PERFORMED BY: EL TEATRO BILINGÜE DE HOUSTON

CARLOS MORTON WILL DISCUSS HIS PLAY AFTER THE SHOW.

Sponsors: Revista Chicano-Riqueña/Arte Publico Press, Cultural Arts Council of Houston, Institute of Hispanic Culture, Ripley House.

Poster, *The Many Deaths of Danny Rosales.*

negative female figure who relates to men in a challenging manner, but ultimately expects her role is to be subordinate to males.

Los Dorados deals with the Spanish conquest of California. In an interesting reversal of stereotypes, this play presents three Spaniards who must face three female Indian women, Amazons, who rule the land. Even though the females are defeated, as were the Indians of California, they are represented as courageous, able to think through their dilemma and ready to take a stand. Tupipe, the survivor, even in her state as a slave, refuses to accept that her children will be so. Her relationship to the Captain is an adversary one where she is physically defeated but spiritually refuses to surrender.

The next two plays stand out for their representation of female-male adversary relationships but with the female in a dominant position. Not surprisingly their author is female, Estela Portillo-Trambley. *Sun Images* is a rollicking musical comedy which seems to be set in leap year! It has several female figures who all seem to be in control of their own lives. Nena, Tita and Tensha are three young women from Mexico who take advantage of Don Estevan to drive them around and to use his house—without allowing him to take advantage of them. Ana, Delfi and Carlos' girl all take the initiative with the boys. Ana tricks Marcos into getting engaged and Carlos is ready to forgive his girl, even though she's had "so many guys in . . . between."

The type of female-male relationships in this play are best summarized in la Melcocha's words:

Men are helpless! They bluster through life creating every kind of trouble. We take care of them, make them comfortable. What on earth would they do without us? I'll have him tame and manageable in no time.

Estela Portillo's other play, and her best known work, *Day of the Swallows,* vividly presents a female character who has turned to homosexuality as a reaction to men whom she finds hateful. Josefa tells Clara: "Men don't love . . . they take . . . haven't you learned that by now?" and Clara retorts with the female dilemma: "Oh, Josefa . . . you are wrong . . . a woman was made to love a man. To love is enough for a woman . . . if only they would let us love them without negating, without negating."

The male characters in this play are almost all hateful, shiftless, double-crossing. Josefa is in control as she dominates her uncle, Tomás, her landlord, Don Esquinas, and even the parish priest, Father Prado. Alysea loves Eduardo and Josefa tries to protect her from the uncertainty and inconstancy of this man's love. She tells Eduardo, "You men explain away all your indiscretions so easily . . . after all, you make the rules and enjoy the abuses!"

In this collection of Chicano plays, I found two that portrayed a female-male partnership relationship. *Brujerías* by Rodrigo Duarte-Clarke and *El Jardín* by Carlos Morton. *Brujerías* is a delightful comedy that satirizes superstitious fears, and in the process presents a humorous but revealing dialogue between a woman and her husband. Doña Petra is a take charge woman who is getting on in years and has grown envious of a neighbor's house. She decides that if Rafael won't help her get a new home, she will take action herself. They throw some derogatory remarks at each other, like, "Have you looked in the mirror recently, you old hag?" "Well, you are no Casanova yourself, you dry stick!" But it all is taken in good spirits. They seem to be comfortable with each other, and there is no evidence that one controls the other.

It seems appropriate to end this survey with *El Jardín,* a parody about Adam and Eve, with God, the Serpent, Columbus, the Church and a Texas Ranger thown in. There is nothing sacred, except God, and many truths and realities are faced. Adam and Eve share their weaknesses and strengths, their views and decisions. Their Chicano identity is the issue and their determination to take action prevails. Eva suggests organization and political action, Adán is prepared to go further if necessary. This is a far cry from *The Ultimate Pendejada.* As Dios says at the end:

> So ends the scene of El Jardín
> A Chicano version of the Fall of Man
> This mixed breed of New World people
> Indian, Spanish, Negro
> Are seeing visions of their own
> Which will someday melt with the dreams of others
> To form a truly Cosmic Race.

Teatropoesía

After surveying this repertory of Chicano plays, the development of *teatropoesía* appears to be a very appropriate female response. As Yvonne Yarbro-Bejarano explains (1983), because of the scarcity of Chicano plays and because scripts are geared to men's perspectives and relegate women to minor parts or stereotyped roles, women have turned to the use of female poetry, which is read and staged like drama. Chicanas are prolific and powerful poets. "In her defiant self-definition, the Chicana writer commits herself to the denunciation of injustice, the injustice of social and economic oppression as well as the unjust imposition of sexual stereotypes" (Yarbro-Bejarano, 1983:88). This strategy of doing theatre is one female answer to the unsatisfactory portrayal of female-male relationships in most Chicano theater thus far.

The rapidity of cultural change and the diversity of attitudes are such in contemporary society that it is unfair to assess the attitudes and perceptions of Chicano theatre or literature, except with the yard-stick of history. But we must face the fact that attitudes tolerated ten years ago, even five years ago! are unacceptable today. Carlos Morton must be commended for his attempt to update his scripts. It is also encouraging to note the adaptability of collectives where female and male input continually modify their theatrical representations to audiences, to time, and to the issues of today's society.

Bibliography

Garza, Roberto J. *Contemporary Chicano Theatre* (Notre Dame: University of Notre Dame Press, 1976).

Kanellos, Nicolás, ed. *Mexican American Theatre Then and Now* (Houston: Arte Publico Press, 1983).

Kanellos, Nicolás and Huerta, Jorge, eds. *Nuevos Pasos: Chicano and Puerto Rican Drama* (Gary, Indiana: Revista Chicano-Riqueña, 1979).

Morton, Carlos. *The Many Deaths of Danny Rosales* (Houston: Arte Publico Press, 1983).

Bibliography